DISTRESS TO DESTINY

Moving From Where You Are To Where You Should Be

Sally Mahihu

Table of Contents

Dedication..V

Acknowledgement..VI

Foreword...VIII

Endorsement..X

Introduction..XI

CHAPTER 1

The Power of Devine Covenant Relationships.........................23

Understanding Your Destiny Relationships

CHAPTER 2

The Power of Relocation...53

From Barrenness and Death to Harvest and Love – The story of Ruth and Naomi

CHAPTER 3

The Power of Prophetic Promise.......................................69

From Deceit and Exploitation to Global Influence – The Story of Jacob

CHAPTER 4

The Power of Positioning...91

From The Cave To The Palace – The Story Of David

CHAPTER 5

The Power of Focus..137

From Slavery and Oppression To Inheritance and Ownership - Story Of Joshua and Caleb

CHAPTER 6

The Power In A Room..159

From Dead Dreams To Resurrected Miracles – *the story of the Shunammite Woman*

CHAPTER 7

The Power Of Choice..173

Your Choices Will Either Keep You in Distress or Move You into Your Destiny

Dedication

I dedicate this book to every person who is in a place of distress in whatever area of life, and who by reading this book will embark on the move from that distress to their place of destiny.

Acknowledgement

For this particular book, I would like to firstly acknowledge my spiritual authority and set man of God, **Reverend Teresa Wairimu,** who birthed me in the spirit and has nurtured equipped and empowered me in the things of God. The content of this Book is largely from the messages she allowed me to preach on the pulpit at Faith Evangelistic Ministry and FEM Family Church, over the years. She has allowed me to tap into the grace that is upon her life and to enjoy the benefits that flow from a spiritual father to a spiritual son.

I thank my husband **Ngari** and my two sons **Eric** and **Chris** for their patience over the years whenever I have "locked" myself away to seek God in the secret place and be immersed in his word, and when I have been away, not only physically, but emotionally in order to pursue my Purpose and Destiny.

I thank the **Ministry team** at Faith Evangelistic Ministry many of whom I found already in the ministry, when I joined and who received me with such love and taught me so much and who have continued to be reference points in my life.

I deeply appreciate my Aunty Reverend Dr **Judy Mbugua** who prayed for me without ceasing for several years so that I could come into the kingdom of God, and who has been a great source of encouragement and inspiration.

I cannot overlook the impact that other **Servants of God** (some who I have never even met) who have impacted me, through their teachings, preaching and authorship.

Finally, everyone who in one way or another, encouraged and provoked me to author this Book.

Foreword

I have known Sally for over 2 decades now, from the time she came to serve me in Ministry when she was still a young wife, mother and lawyer. I am extremely proud that she has turned out to be an incredible woman of God, a seasoned lawyer and a mother not only to her own biological children but to many others whom she has nurtured and mentored over the years. Sally is deeply passionate about the things of God, and in particular with regard to the subject of Destiny which has been one of her favourite themes when teaching. Sally is extremely gifted and anointed in the area of teaching and writing and is a faithful intercessor and a precious gift to the body of Christ and in particular as a minister in the marketplace.

The topics she has covered in this book **DISTRESS TO DESTINY** consist of some of the landmark and defining messages that she has preached on our FEM Ministry platform over the years, and as one can see, they are deeply significant in relation to Destiny.

The biblical characters she has used to illustrate each aspect of these topics gives us the comfort of knowing that these were people like us, who encountered the same issues and challenges that we encounter today. By emulating the principles, they adopted in moving from distress to Destiny, then we can also enhance and accelerate our own journey to destiny. I know every reader will be greatly impacted, equipped and empowered after reading this dynamic book.

Rev. Teresia Wairimu Kinyanjui.

Director& Founder,

Faith Evangelistic Ministry (FEM).

Endorsement

Reading this book by Sally has brought tears to my eyes, because I remember her from when she was literally a small child, and I watched her grow through her teenage years, young adulthood and as she matured into a married woman and most importantly as she accepted Christ as her personal Saviour and zealously embarked on serving God. As Sally often tells people I did intercede for her for several years to come to the knowledge of Jesus Christ.

The manner in which Sally has tackled these deep spiritual topics in this Book is evident of what only God can do through a yielded vessel.

This book will unlock and propel many to their destiny.

Rev. Dr Judy Mbugua.

The Founder of the Homecare Spiritual Fellowship.

Introduction

The dictionary definition of the word "**distress**" speaks of a physical, mental or emotional state of sorrow, pain, suffering, anguish, affliction, torment, misery, desolation, despair, discomfort and stress etc. However, for our purposes in this book we shall expand the definition of "**distress**" to include

…the state of not knowing and not embracing **who** you were born to be namely, your true identity and thereby being in an identity crisis,

…the state of not having discovered and embarked on the **why** you were created namely, your purpose and calling and thereby existing without aim and purpose,

…the state of not having located and positioned yourself at the **where** you were ordained to impact and influence namely, your place and sphere of influence thereby remaining in a wrong place where you can never thrive,

…the state of having identified and connected to the **whom** you were assigned for, namely your right people, relationships, networks and associations, thereby causing you to connect yourself to the wrong people who derail you from your destiny,

…the state of resisting and failing to embrace the **what** it will take to make, mould and shape you, namely your process, thereby hindering you from growing and maturing into the vessel of destiny God intended you to be,

…the state of not having set and established the **which**, namely the principles that will guide you in making your choices and decisions in your journey, thereby causing you to become unstable, double minded and confused, and finally

…the state of giving up and quitting the journey because you have not understood the **that** you will lay hold of, namely the prize after you have paid the price, thereby making you lethargic, passionless and too fatigued to lay hold of your destiny.

To this extent, it is crucial to understand these 7 Ps that will move you from distress to destiny.

1. Moving from Distress to your Destiny will require you to know **YOUR PERSON**; in terms of your true identity and the "**who**" you were born to be. As long as you have **not** come to a revelation and self-discovery of who you are and as long as you have not embraced your true identity, then you will remain in a place of identity crisis and Distress. The key is to understand who God says you are.

   John 15:16 - You did not choose Me, but I chose you and appointed you that you should go and bear fruit, and *that* your fruit should remain, that whatever you ask the Father in My name He may give you.

   John 1:12 - [12] But as many as received Him, to them He gave the right to become children of God, to those who believe in His name.

Genesis 1:27 - ²⁷ So God created man in His *own* image; in the image of God, He created him; male and female He created them.

1 Peter 2:9 - ⁹ But you *are* a chosen generation, a royal priesthood, a holy nation, His own special people, that you may proclaim the praises of Him who called you out of darkness into His marvellous light.

Firstly, the journey to unlocking the passwords to your true identity will entail distinguishing between what should and what should not define you. **Secondly**, identifying and arresting the triggers that often spin you into an identity crisis. **Thirdly**, understanding the voices that seek to define and shape you, so that you may sieve and sift who and what you hear.

When you come to revelation of who you are in Christ you will realize that you were **not** born for distress and that will be the motivation that will empower you to start moving from Distress to Destiny.

Ephesians 2:10 - ¹⁰ For we are His workmanship, created in Christ Jesus for good works, which God prepared beforehand that we should walk in them.

Colossians 3:1-4 - If then you were raised with Christ, seek those things which are above, where Christ is, sitting at the right hand of God. ² Set your mind on things above, not on things on the earth. ³ For you died, and your life is hidden with Christ in God. ⁴ When Christ *who is* our life appears, then you also will appear with Him in glory.

Jacob is a classic example of someone who did not initially understand his true identity and that is why he was in distress for several years until the time he came to a revelation of his true name and true identity and it propelled him to his destiny. (**Genesis 32**).

The "**grasshopper mentality**" in the **children of Israel** caused them to walk in an identity crisis and that is the reason many of them failed to enter their promised land and instead died in the wilderness in distress. (**Numbers 13**).

Joshua and **Caleb** had a revelation of their true identity in a powerful God that gave them a "**giant slayer**" mentality that ushered them to their inheritance.

2. Moving from Distress to Destiny will require you to discover **YOUR PURPOSE**; in terms of your Calling and the "**why**" God created you. Discovering the reason why you are here and what you were created to do, will enable you embark on fulfilling that, Purpose. Without discovering why, you were created and the Purpose you have been called into, means living aimlessly and in distress.

    In addition, even where you may have discovered your Purpose you must be willing to fulfill it effectively and zealously.

    Jere.29:11 - For I know the thoughts that I think toward you, says the Lord, thoughts of peace and not of evil, to give you a future and a hope.

    The minute **Queen Esther** discovered why she was in the palace at that time, led her to discover her purpose and assignment and once she fulfilled it, her and her people were delivered from the distress of annihilation to their destiny. (**Esther 5**).

    The **Shunammite woman** discerned that she had an assignment and a purpose to fulfil by ministering to the servant of God, Elisha, and that discovering and fulfilling her Purpose is what ushered her into her place of miracles and destiny. (**2 Kings 4:8-37 and 2 Kings 8:1-6**).

3. Moving from your Distress to Destiny will entail locating **YOUR PLACE**; in terms of the "**where**" you were ordained to be; the place, sphere, sector, industry and area where God sent you to make a positive impact and transformation as you fulfill your Purpose.

    "Be sure you put your foot in the right place, then stand firm"
    Abraham Lincoln

    Every person has their ordained place and sphere and it is tied to their Purpose and Calling. It is the Place where you will thrive as your gifts, talents and skills manifest and it is the Place where you will be an answer and a solution to problems and dilemmas where you will be celebrated as a game changer.

    Failure to locate and position yourself at your right Place and Sphere means that you will remain in the wrong Place and in Distress, because in the wrong place you will wither and die.

    Deuteronomy 7:1 - "When the Lord your God brings you into the land which you go to possess, and has cast out many nations before you, the Hittites and the Girgashites and the Amorites and the Canaanites and the Perizzites and the Hivites and the Jebusites, seven nations greater and mightier than you.

    Once **Naomi** and **Ruth** realized that they were in the wrong place (namely Moab) which had become a place of death and barrenness and therefore a place of distress, they quickly located their right place, (namely Bethlehem).

    Once they relocated and positioned themselves in Bethlehem, they entered into their place of purpose, promise and destiny.

    Likewise, when God told **Jacob** to return to Bethel, he realized that he had been in the wrong place and that he needed to relocate and be positioned at his place of purpose and destiny. **(Genesis 35)**

4. Moving from your Distress to Destiny will entail identifying **YOUR PEOPLE**; in terms of the "**whom**" you were assigned to walk the Destiny journey with. Connecting to the right relationships, right networks and right associations (namely divine covenant relationships) that will nurture and propel you to your Destiny, is crucial.

    In order to identify whether you have surrounded yourself with the right People and whether you are in the right relationships, you will need to distinguish between your destiny helpers and destiny killers, in terms of who is helping to propel you to destiny and who is derailing you from that destiny.

    Hebrews 10:24-25 - And let us consider one another in order to stir up love and good works, [25] not forsaking the assembling of ourselves together, as *is* the manner of some, but exhorting *one another,* and so much the more as you see the Day approaching.

    David's men (the distressed and discontented debtors) came to a revelation when they identified David as their Set man, and destiny connector, they connected themselves to him in a divine covenant relationship and because they knew he was the one God had ordained to usher them to their destiny.

5. Moving from your Distress to Destiny will entail embracing **YOUR PROCESS**; in terms of the "**what**" you will need to undergo (a molding and a making) to equip and empower you to fulfill your Purpose. Your failure to embrace this Process (which is normally painful) means that you remain in your place of Distress unable to move to your Destiny. In order to ensure that you receive maximum benefit from **Your Process**

of making and moulding, you will need to trust and embrace that process with perseverance and endurance.

Philippians 1:6 - being confident of this very thing, that He who has begun a good work in you will complete *it* until the day of Jesus Christ.

David is a classic example of one who underwent the rigorous regime and process of his moulding and making in the wilderness into the great warrior, leader and king that he became. **David's men** are also a good example of those who embraced the process of their making from distressed discontented debtors into the mighty men of David. **Joseph** had his share of embracing the process that took him from the pit to the palace (by going through Potiphar's house and the prison).

2 Corinthians 4:17-18 - [17] For our light affliction, which is but for a moment, is working for us a far more exceeding *and* eternal weight of glory, [18] while we do not look at the things which are seen, but at the things which are not seen. For the things which are seen *are* temporary, but the things which are not seen *are* eternal.

6. Moving from your Distress to Destiny requires setting and establishing **YOUR PRINCIPLES**; in terms of the "**how**" you will get there. This includes personal values, codes of ethics etc. that you will walk in as you fulfill your Purpose. Failure to establish and set these principles will make you confused and unstable without any foundation on which to base your choices and decisions during crucial crossroads in your journey to Destiny and you will remain in your place of Distress, unable to move on to your Destiny.

Proverbs 11:3 - The integrity of the upright will guide them, But the perversity of the unfaithful will destroy them.

Our journey from distress to destiny will require us to adhere to God's kingdom principles like **David** when he chose to win by righteousness and to trust God's ways and God's timing instead of taking matters into his own hands and killing Saul to get to the palace. (**1 Samuel 24:4-7**)

In other words, like David, we must get to our palace by the hand of God and not by our own carnal methods.

Jacob suffered dearly for overlooking God's principles when he chose to use deception to lay hold of that which was already his instead of waiting for God to hand it to him in God's own way and God's own timing. (**Genesis 27**).

7. Moving from your Distress to your Destiny will require keeping your focus and laying hold of **YOUR PRIZE**; and attaining the **"that"** which is awaiting you after paying the Price (in terms of harvest, successes, rewards, promotions etc.) Failure to lay hold of and manage your Prize, means that you will remain in Distress (despite having come all this way and despite the sacrifices you have made to get here).

This is because your ability to lay hold of your Prize is part and parcel of embracing your Destiny. Paradoxically, it is possible to reach the place where **Your Prize** is awaiting you (in terms of promotions, successes, rewards and harvests), and yet be unable to effectively lay hold of that Prize.

2 Timothy 4:7-8 - I have fought the good fight, I have finished the race, I have kept the faith. [8] Finally, there is laid up for me the crown of righteousness, which the Lord, the righteous Judge, will give to me on that Day, and not to me only but also to all who have loved His appearing.

The **10 spies** and the **children of Israel** who identified with them, were unable to lay hold of their promised land and inheritance even when they physically came into contact with it. The tragedy here is that, even after stepping on that promised land and seeing the evidence of their inheritance, they went back to die in the wilderness, because they were unable to keep their focus on the prize and therefore unable to lay hold of it. (**Numbers 13**)

Fortunately, **Joshua** and **Caleb** maintained their focus on the prize and goal and their faith and trust in God's promises and in Moses the servant of God, enabled them to lay hold of their promised land and inheritance. (**Joshua 14**)

Moving from your distress to destiny will therefore entail you mastering these 7 Ps of knowing and owning your **person**, discovering and fulfilling your **purpose**, locating and positioning yourself in your **place**, identifying and connecting to your **people**, embracing and allowing your **process** to make you, setting and establishing your **principles** and focusing and laying hold of your **prize.**

Having said all this, there are three things that you would still need to address;

Firstly, in order to move from a place of distress to a place of Destiny, you need to understand what your Distress looks like. In other words, you need to ask yourself what tangible factors determine that someone is in a place of Distress, or put in another way what are the symptoms and signs of Distress, examples include fruitlessness, lack of productivity, lack of progress, lack of fulfilment etc.

Your distress can be in any area of your life for example: -

- *In your finances*
- *In your business*
- *In your career and profession*
- *In your health and wellbeing*
- *In your marriage and family life*
- *In your various relationships*
- *In your spiritual life and walk*

As we analyze and take stock of our lives, many of us may come to a place where these elements of distress, fruitlessness, stagnancy and unfulfillment become evident that you are not where you want to be or at any rate you are not where you thought you would be by now.

Secondly, your perception and conclusion that you are not where you should be or where you thought you would be by now, must obviously be based on the assumption that you know where you were supposed to be (either in accordance to God's plan and purpose for your life or by virtue of the dreams and goals you had visualized for yourself). In other words, you can only be distressed by where you are, if you know where you wanted to go.

Thirdly, once you have determined that you are not where you should be, then it becomes incumbent upon you to acknowledge what you might have done or not done, that kept you locked out from where you should be. Then you must diligently seek to understand what you ought to do and zealously embark on doing it, which will often include knowing what choices, decisions and actions you need to take and the principles you need to follow that will move you from your distress to your destiny.

The Bible is full of characters who followed laid down biblical principles that moved them from their distress to their destiny successfully. This book examines these characters and these principles.

For **Naomi** and **Ruth**, understanding the "**power of relocation**" moved them from their distress in Moab to their destiny in Bethlehem. For **Joshua** and **Caleb**, understanding the "**power of focus**" moved them from their slavery and bondage in Egypt to their promised land while those others they were with, died in the wilderness because of broken focus. For **Jacob**, understanding the "**power in a prophetic promise**" delivered him from his distress and his brother's wrath and from exploitation at uncle Laban's, and returned him to his place of promise, purpose and destiny at Bethel. **David and his men** understood the "**power of positioning**" that removed them from their distress in the cave in the wilderness and ushered them into their palace and destiny at Hebron. The **Shunammite woman** understood the "**power in creating room for God**" that lifted her from her distress of childlessness to her place of promise and fruitfulness. In addition, for these and many other characters in the Bible, understanding the "**power of divine covenant relationships**" moved them from distress to destiny and lastly, understanding "**the power of choice**" and how the choices you make will determine whether you remain in distress or move on to destiny.

Psalms 118:5 – "From my distress I called upon the Lord. The Lord answered me and set me in a large place."

This Page Was Intentionally Left Blank

CHAPTER 1

The Power of Devine Covenant Relationships

Understanding Your Destiny Relationships

Chapter Preview

1. *Divine Acceleration Through Divine Connections*

2. *The Fivefold Ministry Will Equip You For Destiny*

3. *Fathers Lay up For Their Children*

4. *Locate Your Father And You Will Locate Your Portion*

5. *Sow Into Divine Connections And Reap A Harvest*

6. *Beware Of Land Mines Created By Your Father's Past Blunders*

7. *The Qualities Of True Spiritual Fathers And True Spiritual Sons*

OPENING REMARKS

Moving from distress to Destiny will require you to identify and connect yourself in divine covenant relationships. The purpose of these relationships is to propel you to Destiny because the right relationships are the engine to Destiny.

Divine Covenant Relationships will include the fivefold ministry, your spiritual fathers and leaders, spiritual mentors, spiritual midwives, destiny helpers such as your burden bearers, your ladder holders, destiny connectors, supporters, sponsors, investors, prophets, intercessors, gate keepers etc.

The relationship is divine because it is God ordained. It is a covenant because it involves agreement between two or more persons with binding obligations and mutually beneficial rewards and outcomes and there is a knitting of hearts and minds.

In understanding the power of divine covenant relationships, there are certain revelations hereunder that you will need to lay hold of in order to make those relationships effective and beneficial in your life. **This chapter focuses mainly on spiritual fathers and authorities.**

In a relay race a wise coach and team manager will put the best runner in the last lap (leg) of the race, a weakness will mess up the whole race. We are the best that God has on the planet earth, the generation that shall finish the race. God has put us on the last leg of the race; Paul, Peter and John are watching us and marvelling and cheering us on.

Hebrews 12:1 – *"Therefore we also, since we are surrounded by so great a cloud of witnesses, let us lay aside every weight, and the sin which so easily ensnares us, and let us run with endurance the race that is set before us"*

We are the **Joshua generation** that will carry the flag and bring down Babylon.

Divine covenant relationships are one of the most fundamental resources you will need, in moving from places of distress to your destiny.

The primary and most fundamental of these divine covenant relationships is the spiritual father – spiritual son relationship which is the main focus of this chapter because all other divine covenant relationships such as your burden bearers, destiny helpers, ladder holders, intercessors, gate keepers, mentors, coaches, sponsors etc. will essentially be connected and aligned to the relationship of spiritual fatherhood and **spiritual** sonship.

As wise people often say *"Spiritual leadership drops something supernatural in your head and life".* Those things come by imitating right.

Spiritual fathers can give you their spirit, like Elisha who got a double portion of the spirit of Elijah. If you follow your leader correctly you will qualify yourself to share in the spirit of that leader falling on your life.

Spiritual leadership will also give you **faith** because when you come into a ministry or into the life of a man of God, you are to follow the faith and not the fashion of that man of God. That faith that God invested in the original calling on the ministry of that leader is to be dispersed into the spirits of each person called to that ministry as they hear the man of God minister and operate in God.

In addition, spiritual leadership will give you **wisdom** from your leader's mistakes. There are two ways that wisdom can be formed in you, firstly when we learn from our own mistakes and we call this **experience**. Secondly when we learn from the mistakes of others, we call this **wisdom**. The difference between the two is that in our own experience we pay for the lessons ourselves whereas wisdom is when another person has paid for the lesson and we just get the lesson free through our followership and association with that leader.

Leaders through their mistakes give us valuable lessons that we do not have to pay for in our lives. To get the wisdom that comes from a father's mistakes you have to practice the sort of intimacy that will make them open that area of their lives to you.

1. DIVINE ACCELERATION THROUGH DIVINE CONNECTIONS

An apostolic and prophetic cover and authority in your life will give you acceleration to your destiny. We stand upon that which our patriarchs did before we came on the scene. We stand on ancient platforms that our spiritual fathers laboured for, the pathways in the spirit that they created for us to have access into the throne room of God in times of need.

Once you make the right connection, what you have been labouring for 20 years, you shall accomplish in 2 days!

Once you identify an apostolic or prophetic cover and source and hook yourself to them, the grace and favour upon that Set man of God will begin to flow in your life and your Calling, Ministry and all the things you have struggled to achieve you will achieve with ease.

When Saul had lost his father's donkeys and had spent several days looking for them, it was when he met with the prophet Samuel (his Set man of God and a spiritual authority) that he received guidance that enabled him to locate those donkeys speedily and to propel him to a place where Samuel would anoint him as the next

King of Israel. In other words, when we encounter the apostolic and prophetic anointing in our Set man of God and in the fivefold ministry, our journey to destiny is accelerated.

1 Samuel 9:19-20 *Samuel answered Saul and said, "I am the seer. Go up before me to the high place, for you shall eat with me today; and tomorrow I will let you go and will tell you all that is in your heart.* ²⁰ *But as for your donkeys that were lost three days ago, do not be anxious about them, for they have been found. And on whom is all the desire of Israel? Is it not on you and on all your father's house?"*

We can enjoy "**spiritual shortcuts**" through divine connections. Jesus didn't tell us to go back and become carpenters and submit under Joseph for 30 years, nor did He tell us to go into the wilderness for 40 days to face the temptations He faced. He had already conquered and destroyed principalities and powers and He was now sending us forth to operate on His own platform that He had laid for us and, in the power, and authority He had obtained for us, hence the reason He said "It is finished"

John 19:30 *So when Jesus had received the sour wine, He said, "It is finished!" And bowing His head, He gave up His spirit.*

Likewise, our spiritual fathers and Set men propel us forward not backwards to pay the same price they have already paid for us. God is doing a quick work in these last days; He intends that we should accomplish his end time purposes in the shortest possible time hence He has ordained shortcuts for us through divine connections.

Elisha was to do twice what Elijah did because Elijah had created pathways for him in the spirit. Elisha understood the power of divine connections, and that is why he connected himself and followed Elijah.

You begin to operate from where the Set Man of God has reached, and above what he has conquered already. You should acknowledge the grace of God placed upon his life that enabled him to get where he has got so you don't have to start from where he started. Instead, you will come to his level and launch on from there.

In the natural our biological fathers laboured for us to get a head-start so we can start from where they had reached, likewise our children will pick up from where we leave and things will be easier for them.

Like Apostle Paul said in Corinthians, parents are supposed to lay up for their children and not the other way round e.g., your children want to be Advocates, Doctors etc. then any goodwill you have created in that profession will benefit them, so they will not have to create a new goodwill, but simply build on the one you left.

The problem of many charismatic believers is insisting on doing things on their own without a father, and insisting on creating their own spiritual pathways instead of enjoying what has already been created by their fathers.

2. THE FIVEFOLD MINISTRY WILL EQUIP YOU FOR DESTINY

We must embrace the fivefold ministry given to us saints by Christ.

Ephesians 4:11-12 *"And He Himself gave some to be apostles, some prophets, some evangelists, and some pastors and teachers, for the equipping of the saints for the work of ministry, for the edifying of the body of Christ"*

God installed the fivefold ministry to equip us saints so that we can handle and operate in those gifts properly. God has positioned the fivefold ministry as his servants to equip you for Destiny.

In (1st Cor. 4:14-18) "*14 I do not write these things to shame you, but as my beloved children I warn you. 15 For though you might have ten thousand instructors in Christ, yet you do not have many fathers; for in Christ Jesus, I have begotten you through the gospel. 16 Therefore I urge you, imitate me. 17 For this reason I have sent Timothy to you, who is my beloved and faithful son in the Lord, who will remind you of my ways in Christ, as I teach everywhere in every church. 18 Now some are puffed up, as though I were not coming to you.*"

Paul writing to his beloved children in the Spirit referred to them as **followers** of him, and told them that he had taught Timothy so that he (Timothy) would in turn remind them of his ways.

(1st Cor. 11:1-2) "*Imitate me, just as I also imitate Christ. Now I praise you, brethren, that you remember me in all things and keep the traditions just as I delivered them to you.*"

Paul was telling them to be followers of him even as he was a follower of Christ: who was our forerunner and who had created pathways in the spirit that Paul located, and he (Paul) overcame the spirit of religion because Christ had broken and put an end to this religious bondage. Timothy had tapped into the grace upon Paul so he could now teach the others.

You may have many instructors, as you move from conference to conference but you must have fathers who will show you pathways in the spirit.

Your fathers will show you how they overcame whatever they overcame e.g., the spirit of prejudice against women preachers was confronted and nullified by pioneers and trendsetters like Kathryn Kulman, Teresia Wairimu and many others so that many women can preach today without prejudice.

There are territories and Nations that were previously impossible to penetrate with the gospel of Christ but our fathers prevailed and conquered those territories and Nations, meaning that you and I can access them, based on the labour and warfare done by our Fathers of pioneering and opening them up.

Romans 4:1 *"What then shall we say that Abraham our father has found according to the flesh?"*

As our descendant, our father Abraham discovered something about God namely that God is a record keeper and every time he believed God it was accounted to him as righteousness. Likewise, any revelation your set man of God has received way before you came on to the scene, is for you to tap into without having to labour for it.

That **Set Man** of God will usher you to new levels of power in the spirit that will change your life forever and enable you to locate your purpose in the master plan of God. Your Set Man is anointed to help you birth out your Purpose and Calling and to usher you to Destiny. Your **Set Man** has the God-given ability to see the talents, skills and gifting within you, and to nurture and harness them, so that you discover and lock into your purpose.

Your **Set Man** will guide you to run your right race in the right lane and to caution you if you begin to veer off. Mordecai was able to guide Queen Esther into understanding her Purpose and into fulfilling it successfully as her **Set Man (Book of Esther)**

Through the word of Knowledge, the **Set Man** will enable you to leap instead of having to crawl.

So, you need a **Father** who will give you instructions of how to reach where you are going, just like Samuel after anointing Saul kissed him (in Greek kissed means equipped) and told him exactly what he would find on the way (**1ˢᵗ Samuel 9**)

Your set man has the word of knowledge and its application specifically for your every situation. Every instruction, counsel and even rebuke from your Set Man is an equipping to empower you for Destiny.

3. FATHERS LAY UP FOR THEIR CHILDREN

In 2nd Cor.12:14 "¹⁴ Now for the third time I am ready to come to you. And I will not be burdensome to you; for I do not seek yours, but you. For the children ought not to lay up for the parents, but the parents for the children."

Paul was telling the Corinthians that he would not be a burden to them because the fathers have responsibility for laying up for their children not the other way round.

God is raising **Fathers** today, not according to chronological age but according to the grace released upon that man, provided he has been a child of the past and as a son to someone, so he now qualifies to be a **father** of the future and a **father** to sons.

So, in other words your refusal and resistance to submit and be fathered means that you disqualify yourself from fathering in the future, because effective **fatherhood** comes from effective **sonship**.

We must learn to uncover and drink from the **Wells** our fathers dug. Isaac renamed the **Wells** exactly the same as his father had named them, he was wise not to change the names. Since his father had already dug the wells years before, Jacob did not need to labour and travail redigging new wells. He simply uncovered and drunk from the wells his father has laboured for.

When we try to bypass the fivefold ministry (Servants of God) and refuse to drink from the **wells** they have dug we are wasting our time, because God positions them there as his Servants to show us where the wells are. Abraham's servant had to show Isaac where the wells were because they were dug when he was a very small boy (**Gen.26:15-22**)

We need to allow these Servants of God to show us where their wells are and their names, so that we don't need to labour –re-digging new wells. A well is a source or storage of water: water symbolises life giving substance, so these wells give us life to fulfil Destiny. So, whatever "Wells" your fathers dug to benefit you, which the enemies of our destiny have blocked and covered up, we have the anointing and authority to uncover and unblock them as we allow the fivefold ministry (servants of God) to guide us.

In addition, we should build upon the resources our fathers left for us. David laid foundations for Solomon for building the temple. David had come and gone and he had made tremendous provision for the building of the temple. He had received the blue print of how it should look like, but he was not the one to build it, so he handed it over to his son Solomon and equipped him to do and finish that which he couldn't. Your Set Man will hand you the baton and mantle so you can finish the race.

David was laying a provision for his son Solomon to work with.

(**1 Chronicles 22:1-5**) *Then David said, "This is the house of the Lord God, and this is the altar of burnt offering for Israel."² So David commanded to gather the aliens who were in the land of Israel; and he appointed masons to cut hewn stones to build the house of God. ³ And David prepared iron in abundance for the nails of the doors of the gates and for the joints, and bronze in abundance beyond measure, ⁴ and cedar trees in abundance; for the Sidonians and those from Tyre brought much cedar wood to David. ⁵ Now David said, "Solomon my son is young and inexperienced, and the house to be built for the Lord must be exceedingly magnificent, famous and glorious throughout all countries. I will now make preparation for it." So, David made abundant preparations before his death.*

The temple would be called the "**Temple of Solomon**" but provision and architectural plans had been made by David. If Solomon had decided to change and do things his own way, God would not have inhabited the temple.

For Jacob when trouble started with uncle Laban, an angel of the Lord began to teach him and show him how God would transfer wealth into his hands, because of the promise God had made him and Abraham and Isaac, his fathers in Bethel, so Jacob was benefiting from those promises.

(Genesis 30:43) *Thus the man became exceedingly prosperous, and had large flocks, female and male servants, and camels and donkeys.*

Genesis 27:10-12 - *Then you shall take it to your father, that he may eat it, and that he may bless you before his death." [11] And Jacob said to Rebekah his mother, "Look, Esau my brother is a hairy man, and I am a smooth-skinned man. [12] Perhaps my father will feel me, and I shall seem to be a deceiver to him; and I shall bring a curse on myself and not a blessing."*

4. LOCATE YOUR FATHER AND YOU WILL LOCATE YOUR PORTION

There are some things with your name on them and when you show up where you are supposed to be, you will possess them automatically, without stress or strive. Focus on locating your place of assignment where you have been sent and ordained to serve and fulfil your purpose and calling. At that place and within that Purpose you will find your spiritual father and set man.

Once you locate your father and **set man** and your place of anointing, which is also your place of assignment, you will locate and lay hold of your portion, your inheritance and your destiny, like Elisha when he located his Elijah, the men of David when they located David, Joshua and Caleb when they located Moses, Ruth when she located her Naomi and many others.

God is working 24/7 trying to reveal our source to us, through dreams, wise counsel and visions, but we are misinterpreting those dreams because we are operating in the flesh instead of in the spirit. It is only in the spirit that we will discern the spiritual. We will discover our purpose, locate our place and identify our set man through prayer and God's word.

Samuel initially anointed and equipped Saul (Kissed him) and gave him a head start through the word of knowledge, but later Saul's disobedience disconnected him from Samuel, (his set man) by thinking he had "**arrived**" and that he therefore didn't need Samuel anymore. The minute Saul disconnected from Samuel he aborted his purpose and Destiny.

(1 Samuel 15:25-29) Now therefore, please pardon my sin, and return with me, that I may worship the Lord." But Samuel said to Saul, "I will not return with you, for you have rejected the word of the Lord, and the Lord has rejected you from being king over Israel." 27 And as Samuel turned around to go away, Saul seized the edge of his robe, and it tore. 28 So Samuel said to him, "The Lord has torn the kingdom of Israel from you today, and has given it to a neighbor of yours, who is better than you. 29 And also the Strength of Israel will not lie nor relent. For He is not a man, that He should relent."

Sometimes your knowledge of God is limited to what you know of your natural biological father, so a time comes when you need to relocate to a spiritual father, who will take you deeper into the knowledge of God. Your natural father may be able to protect you from natural dangers and give you natural things, but you will need a spiritual father to give you spiritual protection and cover and give you a spiritual inheritance.

Your Set Man and Spiritual father has the anointing to do what your natural father is unable and more importantly your Set Man and spiritual Father can undo wrong and negative things imposed upon you by your natural father.

When Jacob was blessing his sons on his death bed, he pronounced a curse on Reuben for defiling his bed. As a result, the Reubenites suffered premature death and lived below their full capacity.

(Genesis 49:3-4) - "Reuben, you are my firstborn, My might and the beginning of my strength, The excellency of dignity and the excellency of power. 4 Unstable as water, you shall not excel, because you went up to your father's bed; Then you defiled it - He went up to my couch.

Years later Moses reversed the curse on Reuben in **Deuteronomy 33:6** - *"Let Reuben live, and not die, Nor let his men be few."*

This changed the destiny of Reuben and the Reubenites forever. Moses used his authority as a servant of God and spiritual authority and father to undo what Reuben's biological father had done.

5. SOW INTO DIVINE CONNECTIONS AND REAP A HARVEST

There are so many believers today carrying burdens which they need not carry. Many are starting to lay their own foundations instead of building on the ones already laid for them by their fathers. Ensure that you are rooted and positioned on the platforms and foundations already laid by your Set Man and spiritual father.

Even Joshua was required to obey and walk in all that God had commanded Moses, he was not given **new** instructions. He was to simply build on what Moses had laid. **(Joshua 1:1-9)**

Your fruitfulness will come as a result of being properly rooted on the right foundations of your fathers.

Your divine covenant relationships will need to be constantly enhanced and strengthened and where there is a breach in any of those relationships either due to recklessness, betrayal, disloyalty, reduced commitment etc. you will need to make every effort to restore those relationships for them to work in your favour.

When we sow into those relationships whether in terms of resources, time, energy, skills etc. we are in essence strengthening those relationships for our benefit and we will definitely reap abundantly from such sowing.

When Abigail provided David and his men provisions when they were in the wilderness (after her foolish husband Nabal had refused to do so and even insulted David) she was in effect sowing into David's life because she discerned that he was the new move of God in Israel at that time and a divine covenant relationship was formed between her and David whereby she became his wife and benefited from the grace and anointing upon his life for the rest of her life.

(1 Samuel 25:39-41) So when David heard that Nabal was dead, he said, "Blessed be the Lord, who has pleaded the cause of my reproach from the hand of Nabal, and has kept His servant from evil! For the Lord has returned the wickedness of Nabal on his own head." And David sent and proposed to Abigail, to take her as his wife. 40 When the servants of David had come to Abigail at Carmel, they spoke to her saying, "David sent us to you, to ask you to become his wife." 41 Then she arose, bowed her face to the earth, and said, "Here is your maidservant, a servant to wash the feet of the servants of my lord."

It is imperative that we learn to sow into our Set man of God, and into the fivefold ministry and our sacrifice in doing so will never go unrewarded.

When Ruth and Naomi reached Bethlehem (after relocating from Moab their place of distress), Ruth was proactive and wise in seeking provision in the fields for her and her mother-in-law, who by now she had recognized was her spiritual midwife and Set man of God.

That diligent act on the part of Ruth reaped her a husband in the name of Boaz and more so it reaped for her a place in the genealogy of Jesus. In short, sowing into your divine covenant relationships can move you from a place of death and barrenness to a place of life and abundance.

6. BEWARE OF LAND MINES CREATED BY YOUR FATHER'S PAST BLUNDERS

In the same way that we can trace our physical features, strengths and weaknesses through our family line is the same way we can trace character traits and flaws in our spiritual fathers that seek to influence us. It is therefore important to understand our spiritual heritage whether good or bad and to recognize the iniquities of our forefathers. This way we can respond to that influence and we can appreciate and celebrate the good that has been passed while acknowledging the iniquities and repenting with a view to overcome the negative tendencies we may have inherited.

While we are not held responsible for the sins of our ancestors, we are susceptible to their areas of weakness and should be alert to these inclinations.

This is found in Exodus 20:5-6; 34:6-7, Numbers 14:18 and Deuteronomy 5:9-10.

In other words what our spiritual fathers do, affects the next generation and we are often deeply influenced by their decisions and the patterns of their lives.

In the days of Nehemiah when they were rebuilding the walls of Jerusalem, Ezra the priest recognized and led the people in repenting for the iniquities of their fathers. *(Nehemiah 9:2 – And the seed of Israel separated themselves from all strangers and stood and confessed their sins and the inequities of their forefathers).*

Jeremiah understood that God's hand of judgement was upon the land and he immediately acknowledged the inequities of their forefathers (Jeremiah 14:20 – *We acknowledge oh Lord our wickedness and the iniquities of our fathers because we have sinned against thee*).

Daniel on his part got a revelation that when the time came for Israel to be restored, he needed to intercede for the sins and iniquities of the fathers and the people. (Daniel 9:1-19)

While locating pathways in the spirit created by your fathers, make sure you don't step or tap into the land mines, that will blow you up.

The hand of strength is also the hand of weakness. There are some bad habits and behaviours in our fathers that we should not tap into. For example, the **"God's Generals"**, volume of Books by Robert Liardon, reveal shocking short comings in great men of God. Avoid past blunders made by your fathers that create potential land mines, that will blow you up and trip you along the way.

In the biblical account of Abraham's family, the iniquity of deception became a stronghold that affected the lives of Abraham, Isaac, Jacob and Jacob's sons (Genesis 12, Genesis 26, Genesis 27 and Genesis 37).

Abraham adopted a deceptive practice when in Genesis 12:11-13 he told a lie about Sarah not being his wife. **(Genesis 12:11-13)** - *And it came to pass, when he was close to entering Egypt, that he said to Sarai his wife, "Indeed I know that you are a woman of beautiful* *countenance. 12 Therefore it will happen, when the Egyptians see you, that they will say, 'This is his wife'; and they will kill me, but they will let you live. 13 Please say you are my sister, that it may be well with me for your sake, and that I may live because of you."*

Later on, Abraham told the same lie in Genesis 20:1-3. **(Genesis 20:1-3)** *And Abraham journeyed from there to the South, and dwelt between Kadesh and Shur, and stayed in Gerar. ² Now Abraham said of Sarah his wife, "She is my sister." And Abimelech king of Gerar sent and took Sarah.³ But God came to Abimelech in a dream by night, and said to him, "Indeed you are a dead man because of the woman whom you have taken, for she is a man's wife."*

Years later the iniquity of deception played a significant role in the lives of Abraham's descendants. Abraham's son Isaac followed Abraham's example and lied about the identity of his wife Rebecca when they travelled in Gerar.

(Genesis 26:7) *So Isaac dwelt in Gerar. 7 And the men of the place asked about his wife. And he said, "She is my sister"; for he was afraid to say, "She is my wife," because he thought, "Lest the men of the place kill me for Rebekah, because she is beautiful to behold."*

Furthermore, in the next generation of Abraham's grandson Jacob (son of Isaac) this iniquity of deception had become entrenched when Rebecca and her son Jacob schemed to deceive Isaac into giving the second born Jacob the blessing of the firstborn that rightfully belonged to Esau.

(Genesis 27:18-19) *- 8 So he went to his father and said, "My father." And he said, "Here I am. Who are you, my son?" 19 Jacob said to his father, "I am Esau your firstborn; I have done just as you told me; please arise, sit and eat of my game, that your soul may bless me."*

Many years later Jacob's sons deceived him concerning the welfare of his son Joseph because they were jealous of the favour Joseph had from Jacob and they sold him as a slave.

(Genesis 37:31-33) - 31 So they took Joseph's tunic, killed a kid of the goats, and dipped the tunic in the blood. 32 Then they sent the tunic of many colors, and they brought it to their father and said, "We have found this. Do you know whether it is your son's tunic or not?" 33 And he recognized it and said, "It is my son's tunic. A wild beast has devoured him. Without doubt Joseph is torn to pieces."

Your Set man of God who is also your spiritual father and authority is someone that God has ordained for you specifically to sit and serve under and who will nurture you, equip and empower you and ultimately usher you into your destiny. To this extent you cannot just sit under anybody just because you like them or they look successful and famous etc.

It is when you are under your right Set man and spiritual authority that the talents, skills and gifting in you will thrive and there will be a cover of protection over you and a gracing to excel.

The devil is legalistic and he holds a remote control waiting for you to blunder or open wrong a door so that he can blow you up. Your **set man** is designed by God to be a gap for you so that you can walk without devils blowing you up. Your set man will point out land mines in your way, so you don't step on them and self-destruct.

The key thing is to take personal responsibility even as you acknowledge the blunders of your spiritual fathers and stop blaming them and instead seek to master your own destiny by recognizing these landmines and blunders and avoiding them because ultimately God will deal with each one of us based on our own actions. **(Jeremiah 31:29-30)** - *29 In those days they shall say no more: 'The fathers have eaten sour grapes, And the children's teeth* *are set on edge.' [30] But every one shall die for his own iniquity; every man who eats the sour grapes, his teeth shall be set on edge.*

In addition, you must beware that when you **deposition** from your right Set man and spiritual authority and you choose to sit and serve under the wrong covering and authority (whether knowingly or unknowingly) then you will not be able to operate efficiently and effectively in your gifting, skills etc.

When Ahitophel, one of King David's trusted advisors made the mistake of depositioning himself from under David and defected to the camp of David's son Absalom who had sought to overthrow David, Ahitophel's ability to operate in wisdom and prophetically became limited and cut off.

(2 Samuel 15:31) Then someone told David, saying, "Ahithophel is among the conspirators with Absalom." And David said, "O Lord, I pray, turn the counsel of Ahithophel into foolishness!"

7. THE QUALITIES OR TRUE SPIRITUAL FATHERS AND TRUE SPIRITUAL SONS

There are certain characteristics, qualities, traits and trademarks of what a true spiritual father is and what a true spiritual son is. There are also very clear roles, responsibilities, mandates, and obligations imposed upon the spiritual father and spiritual son and there is immense value and benefits that flow from this very crucial divine covenant relationship.

There is so much that we need to learn and embrace about this divine concept of spiritual fatherhood and sonship. The principles that determine a true spiritual father and a true spiritual son can greatly assist us in understanding, and walking in this dynamic relationship so as to move from our places of distress to our places of promise, purpose and destiny.

The relationship between a spiritual father and a son is a divinely inspired connection from God between two people and intended for a significant purpose. The father-son relationship is a "**covenant relationship**" between two destiny-oriented individuals, it is not about conferring positions. Authority derived from true fathering is legitimate authority originating from God.

A spiritual father is one who you can have access to anytime in a safe space to share and express our pain and gain with. They have the ability to speak into our lives.

Who is a True Spiritual Father?

1. A spiritual father must have spiritual experience, revelation, knowledge and wisdom arising from his walk with God, and must be able to release them by wisdom to his spiritual sons to guide the son in God's truth, will and purpose.

2. A father's responsibility is therefore more than counselling and mentorship. It is to guide the son in God's purpose. God releases to spiritual fathers that which He wants imparted to the sons. Just as sons in the natural receive an inheritance from their fathers, spiritual fathers lead their sons into their spiritual inheritance.

3. Sons who have been fathered by having submitted to a spiritual father can be released into ministry and can become fathers. Ministers who have no spiritual fathers and covering are without a ministry; and if there is no ministry there is no message.

4. A true spiritual father is characterized by a unique relationship with God. We cannot become a spiritual father by our own decision or effort. No man can make himself a father, except God declares him one because fatherhood is God's initiative.

5. A spiritual father encourages, coaches, and corrects his sons when needed. It is often the voice of a father that is lacking, so when spiritual fathers arise then sons have the confidence and security to step out into the areas God is calling them.

   Paul fathered Timothy: **"Therefore I remind you to stir up the gift of God which is in you through the laying on of my hands"** (2 Timothy 1:6)

True spiritual fathers want to impart and empower sons to walk in their gifts and calling. They are secure enough to make room for them to excel and go beyond their own accomplishments.

Paul guided and encouraged Timothy in his walk with God and his calling as a leader, to stir up the gifts of God.

6. Spiritual fathers pray for their sons. **(2 Timothy 1:3) - I thank God, whom I serve with a pure conscience, as *my* forefathers *did,* as without ceasing I remember you in my prayer's night and day.**

    Just as you pray for your natural children on a daily basis, you have a burden to pray for those who are spiritual children on a regular basis. Perhaps our prayers are the most important thing that we can give to those whom we disciple, mentor, and walk with.

7. Spiritual fathers are loving and affectionate towards their sons. **(2 Timothy 1:2) - To Timothy, a beloved son: Grace, mercy, *and* peace from God the Father and Christ Jesus our Lord.**

    A relationship between a spiritual father and a son/daughter is birthed by God, and there is a true heart connection.

8. A true spiritual father will teach his son how to hear and discern the voice of God, so that the son will mature. The maturity and development of the son lies in the hands of the father as the son walks in submission and relationship with his father. In other words, the father invests in the son to bring him to maturity and greater success, before he can expect to receive. This requires much investment, spiritual deposit and impartation to make, and to see the son become successful and greater. A true spiritual father will find the time to promote and develop the son in order for him to function and come to his place of inheritance.

9. True spiritual fathers imitate God as their son's imitate them. Elijah, Elisha, John the Baptist and Paul are examples of spiritual fathers who were filled with the Holy Spirit, they were single and none had biological children, and yet ironically God's people called them "father" because they "knew" God the Father and imitated him.

10. True spiritual fathers treat others with dignity and respect, they lead and show value to others, they are not demanding, controlling, manipulative, or dictatorial (**1 Thess. 2:6**) - **Nor did we seek glory from men, either from you or from others, when we might have made demands as apostles of Christ.**

They exhibit a heart-felt, compassionate concern for the well-being of the sons.

Paul was gentle toward them (**1 Thess. 2:7**) - **But we were gentle among you, just as a nursing *mother* cherishes her own children.**

He cherished them, he longed for them affectionately (**1 Thess. 2:8**) - **So, affectionately longing for you, we were well pleased to impart to you not only the gospel of God, but also our own lives, because you had become dear to us.**

He not only gave them the gospel, but he gave his own life to them, they were dear to him, he exhorted, comforted, and charged every one of them, as a father does his children (**1 Thess. 2:11**) - **as you know how we exhorted, and comforted, and charged every one of you, as a father *does* his own children.**

He was not interested in shaming them, but did feel obligated to warn them. He was not putting them on a guilt trip or making them feel intimidated, he was not seeking what was theirs (their money), but he was seeking them (**2 Cor. 12:14**) - **Now *for* the third time I am ready to come to you. And I will not be burdensome to you; for I do not seek yours, but you. For the children ought not to lay up for the parents, but the parents for the children.**

11. True spiritual fathers are ethical. They operate within the law of the land, the guidelines of their profession, and the policies of their employer, and most importantly they operate within the principles and word of God.

    They do not seek glory of men or seek to be exalted (**1 Thess. 2:6**) - **Nor did we seek glory from men, either from you or from others, when we might have made demands as apostles of Christ.**

    They do not gather their sons to feed their own ego. They are not covetous toward their sons (**1 Thess. 2:5**) - **For neither at any time did we use flattering words, as you know, nor a cloak for covetousness—God *is* witness.**

    They do not see having a relationship with their sons as a means of getting their goods.

12. **True spiritual father disciplines their sons affectionately and they teach by example;**

    a) First, God the Father is an affectionate disciplinarian, and so are the spiritual fathers who imitate him. It is never either one or the other. It is always both. They do this because this is what our Heavenly Father does. He disciplines the children that he loves (**Heb.12:7-8**)-*If you endure chastening, God deals with you as with sons; for what son is there whom a father does not chasten? [8] But if you are without chastening, of which all have become partakers, then you are illegitimate and not sons*

b) Through his disciple, Elisha, God judged Gehazi's greed, (**2 Kings 5:20-27**). Paul repeatedly warned his spiritual children that, if necessary, he would use his power to discipline the unrepentant (**1 Cor.4:18**) - **Now some are puffed up, as though I were not coming to you.**

Our heavenly Father is also affectionate. God called himself a father to the fatherless (**Psalms.68:5**) - **A father of the fatherless, a defender of widows,** *Is* **God in His holy habitation.**

He is "merciful and gracious, slow to anger, abounding in steadfast love and faithfulness" **Exo.34:6 – And the Lord passed before him and proclaimed, "The Lord, the Lord God, merciful and gracious, longsuffering, and abounding in goodness and truth,**

c) True Spiritual Fathers use discipline coupled with affection and teaching modelled by sincerity and humility.

13. True spiritual fathers act responsibly, they do their duty and are accountable. They own their mistakes and work to do their best in the future.

Spiritual fathers are willing to spend and be spent for their sons, in other words, they are willing to live and give sacrificially for their sons, for their advancement and their development (**2 Cor. 12:15**) - **And I will very gladly spend and be spent for your souls; though the more abundantly I love you, the less I am loved.**

In addition to spiritual fathers, we may have other servants of God in our lives who may not be our spiritual fathers but they play the role of a spiritual mentor (although your spiritual father can also be your spiritual mentor).

A **spiritual mentor** is key and important in our lives because they encourage your spiritual growth. It is someone who cares about you and wants the best for you, they encourage you to invest in your personal relationship with Christ so that you can grow and mature in your faith. They act as a role model because they lead by example and it is not so much the words, they say but their actions that speak louder than words. They guide you by the way they honour God in their choices so that you can do the same.

They believe in you despite your shortcomings by constantly affirming you and encouraging you when you are down and reminding you of your value and relevance, they help you to be accountable and they tell you the truth by pointing out where you may be going wrong and by being accountable to them you are motivated to remain on the right path.

They listen to you when all you need is somebody to hear you without judging you and they allow you to pour yourself out and heal from your struggles.

Most importantly they give you wise counsel during your most difficult seasons and when you have tough choices and decisions to make, they can guide you in the right direction and even caution you against dangers that may derail you from destiny.

Who is a True Spiritual Son?

1. A true son will function like his father. He will emulate his character and his walk with God. Mannerisms and styles can be impersonated, but character comes from observing and walking with your mentor closely. Sons carry their father's legacy and anointing.

2. The difference between sons and "**spiritual enthusiasts**" is submission. Sons do not shy away from commitment and submission to Godly authority. We live in a generation where submission is mistaken for weakness and accountability for intrusion. Submission is not painful or controlling when you trust your spiritual father.

3. Honour is a heart issue and God sees if you are truly honouring a man or not. Many fail to realize that Honour is the bridge God uses to transfer blessings from one generation to another. A spiritual son understands the importance of honouring their spiritual father

4. A spiritual son will out-do and achieve greater successes than their spiritual father. That was Jesus' expectation from his disciples, "He said you shall do greater things…" Success does not mean you are greater or better than your mentor/spiritual father. You can be more anointed, decorated with greater gifts, have a bigger church and still remain a small man. **Humility is the mark of a true son.**

5. As a spiritual son you should give your father regular support as a token of appreciation for their presence in your life. Gifts, financial support, surprises and even a thank you are all an extension of your honour and love for them. Appreciate the

heart that pours into you. Sowing into your spiritual father's life is one of the ways a son demonstrates, that they value their father.

51

The Spiritual Father – Spiritual Son relationship is one of reciprocity and a two-way traffic and process.

This Page Was Intentionally Left Blank

CHAPTER 2

The Power of Relocation

From Barrenness and Death to Harvest and
Love – The story of Ruth and Naomi

Chapter Preview

1. *Reviewing Your Crisis*
2. *Responding at Your Crossroads*
3. *Repositioning in Right Relationships*
4. *Repackaging for a New Beginning*
5. *Reaping in the Right Field*

OPENING REMARKS

The story of Ruth and Naomi as they returned to Bethlehem from Moab is a classic example of the power of relocation in moving you from your place of distress to your place of destiny. Naomi and her husband Elimelech had left their place of purpose namely Bethlehem and they had gone to settle in Moab because they were escaping the famine in Bethlehem.

(**Ruth 1:1-2**) *Now it came to pass, in the days when the judges ruled, that there was a famine in the land. And a certain man of Bethlehem, Judah, went to dwell in the country of Moab, he and his wife and his two sons. ² The name of the man was Elimelech, the name of his wife was Naomi, and the names of his two sons were Mahlon and Chilion—Ephrathites of Bethlehem, Judah. And they went to the country of Moab and remained there.*

They gave their sons in marriage to women of Moab, Ruth and Orpah, but in time Elimelech, Naomi's husband died and so did their two sons leaving Naomi and her two daughters-in-law widowed and childless since neither Ruth nor Orpah had yet conceived and born children by the time their husbands died.

Often, we make the mistake of depositioning ourselves from our right place of purpose and blessing, because of a temporary circumstance and we end up in the wrong place where we cannot thrive. We encounter barrenness and death whether it be physical or in terms of our businesses, careers, relationships etc. and great distress, and at that point we must retrace our steps back to our Bethlehems, symbolizing our real place of purpose and destiny.

Ruth 1:19-22 - Now the two of them went until they came to Bethlehem. And it happened, when they had come to Bethlehem, that all the city was excited because of them; and the women said, "Is this Naomi?" ²⁰ But she said to them, "Do not call me Naomi; call me

Mara, for the Almighty has dealt very bitterly with me. [21] I went out full, and the Lord has brought me home again empty. Why do you call me Naomi, since the Lord has testified against me, and the Almighty has afflicted me? [22] So Naomi returned, and Ruth the Moabites her daughter-in-law with her, who returned from the country of Moab. Now they came to Bethlehem at the beginning of barley harvest.

Relocating from one place to another (especially from a place of adversity) is a crucial step towards moving from distress to Destiny. Relocating will often entail stepping into a **new beginning** i.e., another chance to possess the promises and fulfil the prophetic word that was given to you by God directly or through God's servants or through his written word.

The Word "**new**" implies that you had other beginnings before but for various reasons you did not possess God's promises or at any rate you did not possess them as fully as you had expected, or if you did possess them, God is ushering you into greater promises.

Firstly, it is important to identify what kind of promises you are standing on, which may include; depth in ministry or expansion, business growth-financial breakthrough, healing relationships, fulfilment of a marriage proposal, healing whether physically, emotionally and spiritually, or the recovery or restoration of things that the enemy has taken away or you have lost due to various reasons.

Secondly you must identify the reasons why you may not have possessed those promises e.g., wrong decisions, choices or wrong connections, wrong positioning (not at the right place at the right time), wrong focus, spiritual fatigue, loss of passion and zeal etc.

Thirdly identify what you may need to do differently this time around, in short, in order to relocate successfully and step into a new beginning, you will need to take stock of where you are at and discern where you want to go by examining what held you back in the first place, so that you do not repeat the same mistakes.

A personal stock taking and self-analysis will help you adjust whatever you need to adjust and offload yourself of any burdens and limitations hindering you.

Ruth used five **(5)** **principles** to relocate from Moab (her place of distress) to Bethlehem (her place of destiny)

1. She **REVIEWED** her crisis
2. She **RESPONDED** to her crossroads
3. She **REPOSITIONED** herself in right relationships
4. She **REPACKAGED** herself for a new beginning
5. She **REAPED** in the right field

1. RUTH REVIEWED HER DISTRESS

Ruth found herself in a place of distress and immediately discerned that she was on the cusp of a new beginning and she stepped into it effectively by doing five (5) things that literally propelled her into fulfilling her Destiny and being recorded in the genealogy of Jesus in the gospels of Mathew and Luke.

Ruth reviewed her crisis instead of denying it or allowing it to swallow her, she made a mental calculation and immediately decided that she could no longer remain in Moab. She took charge of the crisis instead of allowing the crisis to take charge of her.

God must have planned Ruth's destiny even before she was formed in her mother's womb.

(Jeremiah.1:5 *"Before I formed you in the womb, I knew you; Before you were born, I sanctified you; I ordained you a prophet to the nations."*)

Everything that happened to her was like a setup by God;

- When Naomi's husband Elimelech made a decision to move his family to Moab it was God's setup no.1
- When Elimelech arranged the marriage of his sons to Moabite women it was God's setup no.2
- When death struck Elimelech and his two sons, it was God's set up no.3
- When Naomi and Ruth decided to return to Bethlehem it was God's set up no.4
- When Ruth went to glean in a field which happened to belong to Boaz, that was God's set up no.5

Sometimes God will orchestrate things in our lives or use the things that happen to us to lead us into exactly where he wants us.

2. RUTH RESPONDED TO HER CRISIS

She responded appropriately to the reality of her situation and her circumstances i.e., widowhood and barrenness. By becoming proactive and taking responsibility (for her future) she didn't wait for someone else to do it. The word "**responsibility**" is made up of two words, "**ability**" and "**respond**".

It is not what happens to us but how we respond to what happens to us that determines our success and failure. She didn't blame the circumstances or anyone, she refused to be a victim of circumstances like her sister-in-law Orpah who failed to respond appropriately and disappeared into oblivion and we never hear of her again.

Victims blame circumstances and other people for their crisis and calamities. Ruth exercised her power of choice. Between something happening to you and your response there is a crucial moment of reflection called the "**power of choice**". Within this brief moment of reflection lies your ability or inability to respond appropriately.

Your response to people who seek to hurt you can either empower them or disempower them depending on how you exercise your power of choice. Also, our response to the bad things that often happen in the course of our journey to destiny will determine whether we move forward, backward or remain stagnant in bitterness, woundedness, offense or other toxic emotion that slowly eat away at you and render you a victim instead of a victor.

Your response will amount to a crucial choice and decision that will shape your life and Destiny. You are where you are today as a consequence of a series of choices and decisions you have made so far. Even failure to make a decision or procrastination is in itself a decision.

Ruth's response to death was to arise and refuse to allow the stench of death to continue weighing her down and her response to her barrenness was to arise and refuse to allow herself to be stigmatized with a negative label.

In that moment she knew that relocating from Moab (the place of death and barrenness) was crucial even though she may not have fully understood what Bethlehem held for her.

3. RUTH REPOSITIONED HERSELF

Moving from distress to destiny will require divine covenant relationships.

Ruth got a revelation of Naomi's value and commitment to her and she knew that Naomi was her divine covenant relationship, her set man and spiritual midwife (despite Naomi's apparent uselessness at that moment)

Ruth's commitment and loyalty to Naomi also paved her pathway to destiny and it was later commended by Boaz i.e., her loyalty paid off because it got her noticed by her Boaz and relocated her into her new beginning. Your response to hopeless circumstances and your decision to remain loyal to your spiritual authority and cover even when it appears that she/he is helpless or valueless is crucial. Ruth chose to cling to Naomi instead of kissing her goodbye like Orpah.

People who disconnect from their spiritual Authority during tough times never enter Destiny. Choosing to remain connected is a personal choice not even your spiritual authority or cover can persuade you or make that choice for you. It comes from a deep revelation about divine covenant relationships and an even deeper revelation of who your spiritual midwife is.

Ruth understood how to reposition herself in the right relationships.

Ruth chose to remain connected to Naomi and to follow her to Bethlehem despite the fact that her connection to Naomi had already been severed by the death of her husband and more so by the fact that she had not born any child with that husband (Naomi's son). So, it was an act of repositioning herself in relationship with Naomi again. By being humble and teachable and remaining submitted to Naomi and obeying Naomi's wise counsel until she laid hold of her Boaz, was also a way of repositioning herself in that relationship with Naomi.

Your Spiritual cover and spiritual midwife are designed to usher you to Destiny step by step. It is a divine relationship that forms a covenant between the two of you and entails roles and obligations upon each of you which are mutually beneficial as long as you each play your part faithfully.

The role of your spiritual midwife is to mentor and counsel you with specific instructions to enable you move from your place of distress to your place of destiny. Naomi was diligent in giving Ruth precise instructions when she sent her to the threshing floor to lie at the feet of Boaz.

Your spiritual midwife knows the right timings and can discern the seasons and precise moments for you to take action and not to take action just like a natural midwife would guide you when to push and when not to push when birthing a physical baby.

Ruth 3:1-9 - *Then Naomi her mother-in-law said to her, "My daughter, shall I not seek security for you, that it may be well with you? ² Now Boaz, whose young women you were with, is he not our relative? In fact, he is winnowing barley tonight at the threshing floor. ³ Therefore wash yourself and anoint yourself, put on your best garment and go down to the threshing floor; but do not make yourself known to the man until he has finished eating and drinking. ⁴ Then it shall be, when he lies down, that you shall notice the place where he lies; and you shall go in, uncover his feet, and lie down; and he will tell you what you should do." ⁵ And she said to her, "All that you say to me I will do." ⁶ So she went down to the threshing floor and did according to all that her mother-in-law instructed her. ⁷ And after Boaz had eaten and drunk, and his heart was cheerful, he went to lie down at the end of the heap of grain; and she came softly, uncovered his feet, and lay down. ⁸ Now it happened at midnight that the man was startled, and turned himself; and there, a woman was lying at his feet. ⁹ And he said, "Who are you?" So, she answered, "I am Ruth, your maidservant.*

Ruth obeyed Naomi her spiritual midwife and she came back and reported to her exactly what had happened. She told her to wait patiently for Boaz to work out the issue.

(Ruth 3:16-18) - *When she came to her mother-in-law, she said, "Is that you, my daughter?" Then she told her all that the man had done for her. 17 And she said, "These six ephahs of barley he gave me; for he said to me, 'Do not go empty-handed to your mother-in-law." 18 Then she said, "Sit still, my daughter, until you know how the matter will turn out; for the man will not rest until he has concluded the matter this day."*

Often our failure to obey and trust the counsel of our spiritual authority and spiritual midwife is what leads us to make painful mistakes and threaten abortion of our destiny.

Your ability to trust and obey your spiritual midwife and authority will be as a result of your close relationship and connection with her as well as your ability to maintain a close and personal relationship with God so that you may remain alert and spiritually sensitive to those right voices (namely the voice of God and the voice of your spiritual midwife).

Ruth obeyed, submitted and trusted so she relocated effectively and successfully from the place of death and barrenness to her new beginning. Lot's wife on the other hand missed an opportunity to relocate from Sodom (wicked Past) to a new beginning because she was too attached to the worldliness of Sodom.

Mrs Lot was double minded and her relationship with God had been distant because it had been through Abraham not direct, and her relationship with her set man Abraham had also been distant. Hence, she lacked the capacity to step into a new beginning, and she lacked sufficient revelation, passion and zeal for Destiny.

If your relationship with God is not direct (but through others) then you will need to get deep and personal with God and also have a strong connection with your set man so as to step into your new beginnings and move from your place of distress to Destiny.

Ruth had already been positioned and connected to Naomi through her marriage to Naomi's son, and his death gave her an opportunity to disconnect because technically the death of her husband set her free, however Ruth chose to **reconnect** herself to Naomi because she discerned that Naomi was her divine destiny connector.

Ruth's decision to remain with Naomi constituted a **reconnection** which was stronger than the first because this time it was not a natural but a spiritual one because she embraced Naomi's God. Ruth discerned that relocating was not automatic and that she needed to **reposition** herself proactively in the right relationships.

Moving from distress to destiny will entail proactivity on your part, radical choices, decisions steps and actions that will culminate in a successful relocation to where you ought to be.

When Ruth married Boaz, she was repositioning herself, this is because, she remained in same lineage as Naomi and family. She deliberately stuck to her initial connection and reconnected through Boaz. The death of Ruth's husband had disconnected her from Naomi and her lineage but marrying Boaz reconnected her to that lineage.

As you step into new Beginning, check if your connection with your Set Man had been broken for whatever reasons and reconnect so that you complete your relocation from distress to destiny.

4. RUTH REPACKAGED HERSELF

By choosing to connect with Naomi and Naomi's God and people, the stigma of being a Moabite began to wear off and Ruth's transformation began. So successful was Ruth's **repackaging** that the people in Bethlehem forgot God's divine law against Moabite women being married by Jewish men.

(Ruth 4:14-17 - *Then the women said to Naomi, "Blessed be the Lord, who has not left you this day without a close relative; and may his name be famous in Israel! [15] And may he be to you a restorer of life and a nourisher of your old age; for your daughter-in-law, who loves you, who is better to you than seven sons, has borne him." [16] Then Naomi took the child and laid him on her bosom, and became a nurse to him.* [17] *Also the neighbour women gave him a name, saying, "There is a son born to Naomi." And they called his name Obed. He is the father of Jesse, the father of David.)*

When you relocate and begin to move from your place of distress towards Destiny certain stigmas, labels, damaged reputations, bad habits, behaviours, shame and reproach will begin to roll and peel off of you and people's negative perception of you will change to a positive perception. You must therefore purpose to repackage yourself by internalizing godly principles and values and making a personal mission statement to guide you as you move from distress to Destiny.

Naomi's instructions to Ruth are valuable lessons for us to learn from as we chose to relocate from our places of distress to our place of destiny.

Ruth told Naomi to: -

a) **Wash** herself (symbolizing a purification, sanctification and consecration)
b) **Anoint** herself – (symbolizing empowerment and equipping)
c) **Change** her garments (symbolizing changed attitudes and mindset etc.)

It is significant that Ruth **repackaged** herself at the threshing floor which signifies a separation process of uprooting anything negative from her past life until only that which is pure and holy remained. The threshing floor is where the wheat was threshed to remove the useless chaff, from the good wheat. Moving from distress to destiny will require us to undergo a threshing floor experience.

Ruth **repackaged** herself adequately and appropriately when she chose the God of Israel and she therefore ended up making a quality decision that ultimately propelled her to her Destiny. Ruth had come to trust the God of her mother-in-law Naomi, a God she did not know. Ruth made a bold declaration in

(**Ruth.1:16-17** *"¹⁶ But Ruth said: "Entreat me not to leave you, Or to turn back from following after you; For wherever you go, I will go; And wherever you lodge, I will lodge; Your people shall be my people, And your God, my God. ¹⁷ Where you die, I will die, And there will I be buried. The Lord do so to me, and more also, If anything but death parts you and me."*)

Ruth made a complete radical shift, physically, mentally, emotionally and spiritually when she chose to follow Naomi. Your relocation must be full and complete not partial or half-hearted.

Ruth was making a very radical destiny choice and decision as she found herself at this new beginning. There was obviously a risk involved in Ruth's decision, but Destiny decisions are often risky anyway. Ruth's decision was risky because of the possible rejection in Bethlehem since she was a Moabite and hence a foreigner and outsider, who was from a people who worshipped idols.

Destiny decisions always have risks of moving into the unknown. Orpah feared the unknown, and settled for the less risky path and ended up irrelevant, but Ruth took the risk and got eternal security as she entered her Destiny, and left a significant legacy for future generations.

Our decisions and choices often have the power to affect many other people whether positively or negatively.

Ruth's decision was motivated by her desire to know the true God of Israel as her God which was a defining moment of breaking away and disconnecting herself from *chemosh* of *Moab* (the idol god). It is possible that Ruth got a revelation that the idol gods of Moab had not helped her so far and perhaps the God of Ruth would help her break her barrenness.

In addition, Ruth **repackaged** herself when she obeyed and heeded Naomi's wise instructions even when those instructions made her act unconventionally. Ruth realized that Naomi understood the culture at Bethlehem which Ruth did not and hence the reason why she chose to trust her.

5. RUTH REAPED IN THE RIGHT FIELD

Ruth 2:2-9 - *² So Ruth the Moabitess said to Naomi, "Please let me go to the field, and glean heads of grain after him in whose sight I may find favor." And she said to her, "Go, my daughter." ³ Then she left, and went and gleaned in the field after the reapers. And she happened to come to the part of the field belonging to Boaz, who was of the family of Elimelech. ⁴ Now behold, Boaz came from Bethlehem, and said to the reapers, "The Lord be with you!" And they answered him, "The Lord bless you!" ⁵ Then Boaz said to his servant who was in charge of the reapers, "Whose young woman is this?" ⁶ So the servant who was in charge of the reapers answered and said, "It is the young Moabite woman who came back with Naomi from the country of Moab. ⁷ And she said, 'Please let me glean and gather after the reapers among the sheaves.' So, she came and has continued from morning until now, though she rested a little in the house." ⁸ Then Boaz said to Ruth, "You will listen, my daughter, will you not? Do not go to glean in another field, nor go from here, but stay close by my young women. ⁹ Let your eyes be on the field which they reap, and go after them. Have I not commanded the young men not to touch you? And when you are thirsty, go to the vessels and drink from what the young men have drawn."*

It is significant to note that Ruth relocated to Bethlehem during spring time which symbolized new life, new beginning and showers of blessings. This shows that by virtue of her quality choices and decisions Ruth literally stepped into a harvest where she initially gleaned the fields and eventually owned those same fields when she married Boaz.

Ruth had not sown yet she reaped a mighty harvest and a mighty destiny. This goes to show that when we align ourselves with the right principles of relocation we shall reap where we have not sown.

Ruth may not have sown in the Barley of harvest but she had sown in her spiritual midwife Naomi. The reason why Boaz noticed Ruth in the first place was because of the rumours about her commitment to Naomi

Ruth 2:11-12 - *And Boaz answered and said to her, "It has been fully reported to me, all that you have done for your mother-in-law since the death of your husband, and how you have left your father and your mother and the land of your birth, and have come to a people whom you did not know before. [12] The Lord repays your work, and a full reward be given you by the Lord God of Israel, under whose wings you have come for refuge.*

Boaz commented on how Ruth deserved to be rewarded for her commitment and loyalty to Naomi. Boaz was so impressed that he favoured her with special protection and provision, (extra sheaves to glean and roasted grain). Ruth's loyalty to her Naomi, her set man opened doors for her Boaz.

Ruth 2:14-17 - *Now Boaz said to her at mealtime, "Come here, and eat of the bread, and dip your piece of bread in the vinegar." So, she sat beside the reapers, and he passed parched grain to her; and she ate and was satisfied, and kept some back. [15] And when she rose up to glean, Boaz commanded his young men, saying, "Let her glean even among the sheaves, and do not reproach her. [16] Also let grain from the bundles fall purposely for her; leave it that she may glean, and do not rebuke her." [17] So she gleaned in the field until evening, and beat out what she had gleaned, and it was about an ephah of barley.*

It is also significant to note that when Ruth arrived in Bethlehem, she set to work in the fields symbolizing that for our move from distress to destiny to be successful, we must be found busy in the vineyard of the Lord. God ordered Ruth's steps into just the right fields where she found the right people.

Her favour came when she was seen by the right people namely Boaz. Once we relocate to our right place, we will also find our right people who will usher us to our miracles and ultimately to our destiny.

There are two crucial lessons we learn here:

I) Your remaining connected and loyal to your set man has rewards that will open doors into your miracles and destiny.

II) When you arrive at your new location and step into your new beginning and begin to receive blessings (roasted grain) like Ruth, remember your set man and midwife. Ruth could have abandoned Naomi once she reached Bethlehem and she could have decided to serve her own interests but instead she remained connected to her spiritual midwife.

Ruth 2:18-19 - *Then she took it up and went into the city, and her mother-in-law saw what she had gleaned. So, she brought out and gave to her what she had kept back after she had been satisfied. ¹⁹ And her mother-in-law said to her, "Where have you gleaned today? And where did you work? Blessed be the one who took notice of you." So, she told her mother-in-law with whom she had worked, and said, "The man's name with whom I worked today is Boaz."*

We must be alert in the spirit to recognize when God is giving us new beginnings and to step into them swiftly and relocate from our place of distress to our place of destiny.

CHAPTER 3

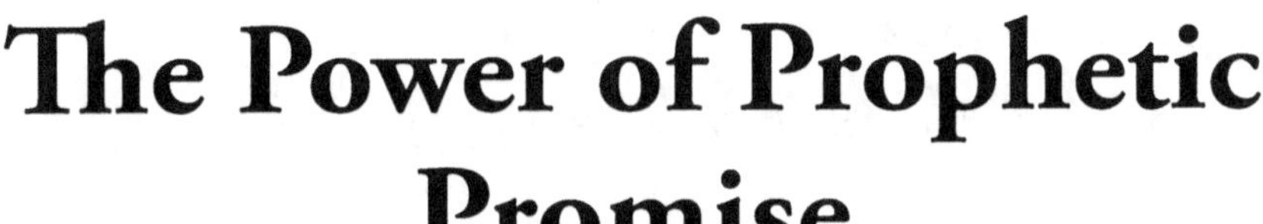

The Power of Prophetic Promise

From Deceit and Exploitation to Global
Influence – The Story of Jacob

Chapter Preview

1. *Your Birthing Comes with a Prophetic Promise*

2. *Your Ladder Experience*

3. *Your Season at Uncle Laban's*

4. *Your Exit from Uncle Laban's*

5. *Your Peniel Experience*

6. *Your Confrontation with Your Esau*

7. *Your Season at Shechem*

OPENING REMARKS

One of the things God does when He begins to move us from distress to destiny is to revisit his promises to us. When there is a word, a promise, or a prophecy over your life that God gave you, which has not yet manifested or come to pass, you may reach a point where you are doubting God's promises and you find yourself in a place of distress. Yet if you choose to have faith and trust God as the promise keeper, then a time will come when God will begin to revisit His word and promise over your life.

At the right time God remembers every word and promise He has ever given you and begins to fulfil it. God remembered the promise He had made to Sarah, to Jacob, to Noah, to the children of Israel etc. He is a promise keeper who remembers all his covenants to fulfil them.

(Jeremiah 1:12) *Then the Lord said to me, "You have seen well, for I am ready to perform My word."*

The important thing therefore is to ensure that we are well-positioned and spiritually alert when God gets ready to remember and revisit His promises to us. Jacob underwent seven (7) significant stages from his birth to his returning to his place of promise as God revisited his promise and word over him. (Genesis 25-35). These 7 stages form valuable lessons for us as we seek to move from distress to destiny.

1. **YOUR BIRTHING COMES WITH A PROPHETIC PROMISE (GENESIS 25)**

His birth was as a consequence of broken barrenness through prayer, when Isaac prayed for his wife Rebekah.

Genesis.25:21 "Now Isaac pleaded with the Lord for his wife, because she was barren; and the Lord granted his plea, and Rebekah his wife conceived."

Isaac himself had been a product of broken barrenness.

It is interesting that those carrying great destinies will often be born after the breaking of a stubborn barrenness or after the making of a bold vow like Hannah made for Samuel. A child of destiny often comes forth through prayers that have the power to break barrenness.

Likewise, the birthing of your purpose, calling and destiny will come through the prayers of an anointed authority over you. Just like Isaac was an authority over his wife Rebekah. Eli the priest decreed over Hannah and her barrenness was broken

(1 Samuel 1:17) - Then Eli answered and said, "Go in peace, and the God of Israel grant your petition which you have asked of Him."

Barrenness signifies hardness and dryness, so the prayers will involve an effectual fervency and a deep travailing like birth pangs, in the place of prayer to pave way for the conception of your prophetic promise and the safe carrying of that promise.

The birthing will also require prayer from a place of aggressive desperation, because it is one thing to conceive and carry your prophetic promise but yet another thing to birth it successfully. Just like Jacob pushed his way out of his mother's womb you will also need to push your prophetic promise and purpose out of you when the time comes. Like Jacob, birthing your prophetic purpose and promise will entail contention and a fierce determination.

(Matthew 11:12) And from the days of John the Baptist until now the kingdom of heaven suffers violence, and the violent take it by force.

God had already chosen Jacob to prevail over Esau while he was still in his mother's womb, meaning that the birth-right would come through God's hand not by the manipulation of man's hand.

Genesis 25:23 - And the Lord said to her: "Two nations are in your womb, Two peoples shall be separated from your body; One people shall be stronger than the other, And the older shall serve the younger."

Yet Jacob chose to use his flesh in his haste to accelerate this promise, by trying to help God so he ended up threatening and risking his destiny, by causing enemity between him and his brother Esau that led to a self-inflicted exile to a place of distress.

Jacob's deception and conmanship led him to flee and thereby deposition himself from the place of promise and purpose for several years before he could return to his place of promise and purpose where he needed to be positioned for God's promise to be fully manifested and fulfilled.

Genesis 27:6-8 - So Rebekah spoke to Jacob her son, saying, "Indeed I heard your father speak to Esau your brother, saying, 7 'Bring me game and make savory food for me, that I may eat it and bless you in the presence of the Lord before my death.' 8 Now therefore, my son, obey my voice according to what I command you.

His mother Rebekah's involvement in the deception is a warning about insensitive spiritual authority who may seek to push your vision out before time carnally in the flesh. Your spiritual authority and spiritual midwife must be a one who hears God and who trusts God enough to teach you how to await the right timing and to let God do things his way.

Often, we go ahead of God's timing and we try to manipulate to get what is already ours (just like Sarah and Abraham who got impatient and birthed an Ishmael or King Saul who offered sacrifices in disobedience and impatience and aborted his destiny). Whenever we seek to handle the prophetic promise over our life carnally or in the flesh we will end up in a place of distress.

God had already revealed to Rebekah that she had "**two nations**" in her womb.

(Genesis 25:23-26) - And the Lord said to her: "Two nations are in your womb, Two peoples shall be separated from your body; One people shall be stronger than the other, And the older shall serve the younger." 24 So when her days were fulfilled for her to give birth, indeed there were twins in her womb. 25 And the first came out red. He was like a hairy garment all over; so, they called his name Esau. 26 Afterward his brother came out, and his hand took hold of Esau's heel; so his name was called Jacob. Isaac was sixty years old when she bore them.

He had already made it clear who His preference was (Jacob) so she simply needed to trust God and let him work it out in His own way and in His own time. Symbolically for us when we are birthed in Christ through salvation, we become partakers of God's promises and his intention is to fulfil each and every one of those promises. Even where it may appear that it has taken too long or we have aborted those promises, God is always faithful to revisit His word and promises to fulfil them provided we position ourselves correctly and do our part.

2.   YOUR LADDER EXPERIENCE AT BETHEL

(Genesis 28:10-15) - Now Jacob went out from Beersheba and went toward Haran. 11 So he came to a certain place and stayed there all night, because the sun had set. And he took one of the stones of that place and put it at his head, and he lay down in that place to sleep. 12 Then he dreamed, and behold, a ladder was set up on the earth, and its top reached to heaven; and there the angels of God were ascending and descending on it. 13 And behold, the Lord stood above it and said: "I am the Lord God of Abraham your father and the God of Isaac; the land on which you lie I will give to you and your descendants. 14 Also your descendants shall be as the dust of

the earth; you shall spread abroad to the west and the east, to the north and the south; and in you and in your seed all the families of the earth shall be blessed. 15 Behold, I am with you and will keep[a] you wherever you go, and will bring you back to this land; for I will not leave you until I have done what I have spoken to you."

Jacob encountered God on his way to Laban's and a covenant was made between him and God as Jacob raised an altar unto God there and God gave Jacob promises which He would later revisit and fulfil years later. God will often give us a promise and then we find ourselves in the wilderness, facing trials, tribulations and fiery furnaces.

This is because we must undergo the process of moulding and making before the promise is fulfilled and manifested, because we must be matured to ensure that we can handle the magnitude and greatness of that promise.

Perhaps God gives us the promise to enable us survive the wilderness with something to hold on to, so that we don't give up. The promise remains as our incentive and motivation to endure and persevere and it gives us a reason to embrace the process of our making knowing that it has a purpose.

3. YOUR SEASON AT LABAN'S (GENESIS 29-31)

After tricking Esau his brother out of the birth-right, Jacob had to flee to his uncle Laban's because of Esau's wrath and revenge.

Genesis 27:42-45 - *And the words of Esau her older son were told to Rebekah. So, she sent and called Jacob her younger son, and said to him, "Surely your brother Esau comforts himself concerning you by intending to kill you. 43 Now therefore, my son, obey my voice: arise, flee to my brother Laban in Haran. 44 And stay with him a few days, until your brother's fury turns away, 45 until your brother's anger* *turns away from you, and he forgets what you have done to him; then I will send and bring you from there. Why should I be bereaved also of you both in one day?"*

Jacob ends up at his uncle Laban's because of his poor choices and carnal behaviour. Laban's place symbolises a place of distress, oppression, bondage, idolatry, exploitation, labour without just rewards, a place of severe trials, tribulations and the painful place of your making. It also symbolizes a place where you get a taste of your own medicine. Jacob experienced being deceived and short-changed by his uncle Laban when he gave him the wrong daughter Leah as a bride in the dark instead of his first choice Rachel and Jacob had to work another 7 years for his first choice Rachel

Genesis 29:23-28 - *Now it came to pass in the evening, that he took Leah his daughter and brought her to Jacob; and he went in to her. [24] And Laban gave his maid Zilpah to his daughter Leah as a maid. [25] So it came to pass in the morning, that behold, it was Leah. And he said to Laban, "What is this you have done to me? Was it not for Rachel that I served you? Why then have you deceived me?"*

[26] And Laban said, "It must not be done so in our country, to give the younger before the firstborn. [27] Fulfill her week, and we will give you this one also for the service which you will serve with me still another seven years." [28] Then Jacob did so and fulfilled her week. So, he gave him his daughter Rachel as wife also.

God's hand was upon Jacob all that time he was at Laban's place, but even though there was some measure of prosperity, it was nowhere near what God had promised him, and to that extent Laban's place was a place of distress for Jacob.

Laban's place is a dangerous place because you may be deceived to settle for less than what God had promised you, and thereby abort your real Destiny. People may convince you that all is well at Laban's since you appear to be doing "okay" but deep within you, you know better, and you know that Laban is not your real destination, because you must return to your real place of destiny.

It is imperative upon you to know your reality, and not walk in self-deception as to where you really are lest you mistake a place of distress as a place of destiny. It is crucial to know yourself and your destiny so that people do not deceive you into settling for less than your real Destiny. Elkanah, Hannah's husband kept convincing her that she should settle for him instead of yearning to birth her Samuel, but Hannah knew better and she refused to settle for less than what she knew God had for her.

1 Samuel 1:8 *Then Elkanah her husband said to her, "Hannah, why do you weep? Why do you not eat? And why is your heart grieved? Am I not better to you than ten sons?"*

So, remember that Laban's place is not your destination, it is a slippery stepping stone to your destiny and you must be careful not to fall and remain crippled there. It is a holding position for God to make and mould you. Even though God may not have intended Jacob to mess and end up at uncle Laban's, nonetheless God used the season at Laban's to transform Jacob from a trickster into a man of destiny.

4. YOUR EXIT FROM UNCLE LABAN'S (GENESIS 31)

You must discern when your season at Laban's expires, so that you strategize your exit plan and leave. Beware that Laban's place does not become a comfort zone-where you begin to get used to and normalize your pain, frustration and disappointment until you lose any incentive to exit and leave. Beware you don't begin to silence and kill your passion and zeal for your destiny.

You will know that your season at Laban's has come to an end when: -

The Labanites begin to murmur against you

Genesis 31:1-2 - *Now Jacob heard the words of Laban's sons, saying, "Jacob has taken away all that was our father's, and from what was our father's he has acquired all this wealth." ² And Jacob saw the countenance of Laban, and indeed it was not favorable toward him as before.*

A time may come whether in your workplace, family, church or community when those who previously accepted and received you begin to reject you and find fault in you and that place becomes a place of distress and you know it is time to exit and go where you will be celebrated and not merely tolerated. Jacob became a stench and a threat to the sons of Laban and to Laban and a target of their envy and jealousy and he knew that it was his time to exit Laban's.

You become restless, discontented and dissatisfied. Even beyond any murmurings or any rejections, sometimes you may just sense that you have outgrown the place you are at. You no longer feel challenged because you have exhausted your potential in that place or you have matured sufficiently in terms of character, skills and competence. You must move on, otherwise you will die in mediocrity, and miss what God has for you at your next level.

You begin to remember God's promise and word over you. A time comes when the prophetic promises given to you years ago begin to stir in your spirit and you begin to yearn for their fulfilment. God begins to sensitize you in the spirit of his intention to revisit his word and promise over you.

This is what happened to Jacob and he purposed to arise and pursue his promises. In addition, God spoke to Jacob and instructed him that it was time to exit Laban's and return his place of promise where God would fulfil His word.

God knows when your seasons need to change and failure to hear Him and exit a season that is ending in your life in order to enter a new season will lead you to stagnation and sorrow and you will remain in a place of distress.

Genesis 31:3 - *Then the Lord said to Jacob, "Return to the land of your fathers and to your family, and I will be with you."*

God's instructions are never up for discussion, you do not need to begin discussing your exit plan with Laban, you should just obey God's instruction and exit promptly.

Even after Laban discovers your exit plan and pretends that it is okay, do not believe him and do not adopt Laban's language. When Laban told Jacob they make a covenant he tried to manipulate Jacob by using the Aramaic language which praised Laban's idol gods but notice how Jacob used the Hebrew language that praised his true God

Genesis 31:44-47 - Now therefore, come, let us make a covenant, you and I, and let it be a witness between you and me." ⁴⁵ So Jacob took a stone and set it up as a pillar. ⁴⁶ Then Jacob said to his brethren, "Gather stones." And they took stones and made a heap, and they ate there on the heap. ⁴⁷ Laban called it Jegar Sahadutha, but Jacob called it Galeed.

As we move from distress to destiny our **"language"** must be that which is aligned to the truth and will of God because our words are powerful and they can make or break us. They can steer us towards destiny or away from destiny.

So, beware of Laban's manipulation even at the last minute when you know you must exit that place of distress.

5. YOUR PENIEL EXPERIENCE (GENESIS 32)

As Jacob began returning to Bethel his place of promise, he encountered God again at Peniel **(Genesis 32:22-32)** and they engaged in an intense wrestling the whole night. It is interesting to note that Jacob separated himself from his wives, children and servants so that he was left alone, signifying that our deepest and most intense moments with God will be when we are alone in a place of separation.

(Genesis 32:22-24) *And he arose that night and took his two wives, his two female servants, and his eleven sons, and crossed over the ford of Jabbok. ²³ He took them, sent them over the brook, and sent over what he had. ²⁴ Then Jacob was left alone; and a Man wrestled with him until the breaking of day.*

The wrestling symbolized Jacob's desperation to lay hold of his promise and destiny, and a fierce determination by Jacob to end his years of turmoil and distress and come to a place of rest and destiny. Our ability to enter destiny from distress will often be dependent on how desperately we actually want it.

God was ready to revisit his word and promise over Jacob because he had really been transformed through the process of his making, and this wrestling encounter was clear evidence of just how determined Jacob was to prevail and succeed. Jacob had come to a place of revelation that he needed to hold on to God stubbornly (symbolizing a committed close walk and connection to God) in order to receive his promises.

God needed to check that Jacob had been well moulded during the process in the wilderness of Padan Aram (uncle Laban's) and whether he had matured enough to receive the promises God had made to him. We need to come to a place of intense wrestling with God with regard to every area of our lives (like Jacob) in order to lay hold of the promises God has made to us.

If the promises manifest before the moulding and making process, we may not value those promises and we may not be able to handle them maturely and use them for the purposes God intended.

Our character and mind-set must be moulded, our gifts must be sharpened and harnessed and our motives and agendas must be tested and purged to equip and empower us for God's promises to be revisited in our lives.

Two significant things happened at Peniel

Firstly, God gives Jacob a new name (Israel) to signify that Jacob had indeed been transformed and the previous negative connotations, stigmas and negative labelling attached to his name Jacob would no longer define him.

(Genesis 32:28) *And He said, "Your name shall no longer be called Jacob, but Israel; for you have struggled with God and with men, and have prevailed."*

Secondly, the wrestling left Jacob with a limp that would forever humble him and remind him of this encounter.

(Genesis 32:31) *Just as he crossed over Peniel the sun rose on him, and he limped on his hip.*

This tells us that when God is moving us from distress to destiny, he will often give us a new name and identity and a humbling limp to remind us that we cannot do it on our own and that we must have a real encounter with Him to qualify for destiny.

6. YOUR CONFRONTATION WITH YOUR ESAU (GENESIS 33)

Esau symbolizes your past fears, past failures, mistakes, poor choices, shame and reproach, zeal without knowledge. Esau also symbolises unresolved issues in your life that you must confront and make right before returning and entering your place of promise from your self-inflicted exile in the wilderness.

In addition, Esau symbolizes your past carnal life when you operated in the flesh because you did not trust God enough to let Him fulfil the promises He gave you, so encountering and confronting Esau means overcoming your flesh, your fears and your painful past as you move from your place of distress to your place of Destiny.

Jacob's Peniel experience had equipped and empowered him with the right name and identity, wisdom and godly authority and hence the reason he was able to come out victorious after his confrontation with Esau.

It is important to note that even though Jacob had to confront Esau before he could enter his place of promise and destiny, nonetheless, he was very careful to remain disconnected and separated from Esau and hence the reason he rejected Esau's two offers.

(Genesis 33:14-16) - Please let my lord go on ahead before his servant. I will lead on slowly at a pace which the livestock that go before me, and the children, are able to endure, until I come to my lord in Seir." ¹⁵ And Esau said, "Now let me leave with you some of the people who are with me." But he said, "What need is there? Let me find favor in the sight of my lord." ¹⁶ So Esau returned that day on his way to Seir.

This signifies that healing from your past does not mean returning to live in and with that past. Esau represents your regrettable past so even as you make peace with it you must let it go and move on to your future. Accepting Esau's offers would have bound Jacob to his undesirable past.

We often make the mistake of thinking that forgiving and reconciling our differences with those we have wronged or have wronged us, means restoring those relationships, but there are some relationships that you should not seek to restore because they are no longer part of your future and they must remain in your past.

7. YOUR SEASON AT SHECHEM (GENESIS 35)

Jacob finds himself at Shechem on his to Bethel way to his place of promise, and he told his family to get rid of all the foreign gods, to purify and change their clothes.

(Genesis 35:1-5) *Then God said to Jacob, "Arise, go up to Bethel and dwell there; and make an altar there to God, who appeared to you when you fled from the face of Esau your brother." ² And Jacob said to his household and to all who were with him, "Put away the foreign gods that are among you, purify yourselves, and change your garments. ³ Then let us arise and go up to Bethel; and I will make an altar there to God, who answered me in the day of my distress and has been with me in the way which I have gone." ⁴ So they gave Jacob all the foreign gods which were in their hands, and the earrings which were in their ears; and Jacob hid them under the terebinth tree which was by Shechem. ⁵ And they journeyed, and the terror of God was upon the cities that were all around them, and they did not pursue the sons of Jacob.*

Before Jacob could return to Bethel, he needed to first forsake all the idolatry that he had become entangled with while at Laban's. Raising an altar for God signified reinforcing his allegiance and relationship with God which required that he burn and bury every idol in his life. The purification and change of clothes signified a sanctification and a consecration.

Our moving from a place of distress to a place of destiny will entail a radical forsaking of every idol in our lives whether it be ungodly and empty relationships, obsession with material substance, carnal wants and desires, vain positions of power, social status etc.

Shechem was about a day's journey from Jacob's appointed destination in Bethel, but he settled there for some time although God's instruction was categorical that he was to go to Bethel. Jacob's decision to pause at Shechem was made in the flesh because Shechem was a "**convenient choice**" where things went well at first and he enjoyed lucrative trading opportunities and even bought land

(Genesis 33:18-20) *Then Jacob came safely to the city of Shechem, which is in the land of Canaan, when he came from Padan Aram; and he pitched his tent before the city. ¹⁹ And he bought the parcel of land, where he had pitched his tent, from the children of Hamor, Shechem's father, for one hundred pieces of money. ²⁰ Then he erected an altar there and called it El Elohe Israel.*

However, this convenient choice was a deception and it had tragic long-term consequences following the conflict between Jacob's family and the Shechemites when Jacob's daughter Dinah was raped by Shechem a member of the ruling Canannite family.

Genesis 34:1-7 - Now Dinah the daughter of Leah, whom she had borne to Jacob, went out to see the daughters of the land. ² And when Shechem the son of Hamor the Hivite, prince of the country, saw her, he took her and lay with her, and violated her. ³ His soul was strongly attracted to Dinah the daughter of Jacob, and he loved the young woman and spoke kindly to the young woman. ⁴ So Shechem spoke to his father Hamor, saying, "Get me this young woman as a wife." ⁵ And Jacob heard that he had defiled Dinah his daughter. Now his sons were with his livestock in the field; so, Jacob held his peace until they came. ⁶ Then Hamor the father of Shechem went out to Jacob to speak with him. ⁷ And the sons of Jacob came in from the field when they heard it; and the men were grieved and very angry, because he had done a disgraceful thing in Israel by lying with Jacob's daughter, a thing which ought not to be done.

The rape of Jacob's daughter at Shechem became a great distress which demonstrates that when we are moving from distress to destiny we often mess up and delay our move and entry into our promises and destiny by prolonging our stay in distress or creating new places of distress that were not supposed to be there. Furthermore, the aftermath caused by Jacob's sons as they revenged against the Shechemites led to even worse messes and more distress.

Genesis 34:25-27 *Now it came to pass on the third day, when they were in pain, that two of the sons of Jacob, Simeon and Levi, Dinah's brothers, each took his sword and came boldly upon the city and killed all the males. [26] And they killed Hamor and Shechem his son with the edge of the sword, and took Dinah from Shechem's house, and went out. [27] The sons of Jacob came upon the slain, and plundered the city, because their sister had been defiled.*

Moving from your distress to your destiny will therefore require prompt and full obedience and trust in God's instructions. Shechem symbolizes and represents our tragic convenient choices which we make when we fail to obey God's instructions in full but partially.

Shechem also represents tragic temptations that seek to ensnare us on the eve of our breakthrough (Jacob was literally one day's journey away from where he should have been). So, beware that you do not settle at Shechem because it means settling for less than the full promises God has for you at your appointed place.

Jacob raises an altar at Bethel again like he had done during his last encounter with God and it is this raising an altar again that provokes God to revisit his promise to him. In Jacob's days raising an altar meant erecting an actual physical structure.

For us today raising an altar to God is symbolic and involves our sacrificial service to God, sacrificial offerings, our prayers and fasting which are all intended to strengthening our relationship with God. The physical altars in Jacob's time often needed to be rebuilt and restored because over time they would break down

(Genesis 35:6-7) *So Jacob came to Luz (that is, Bethel), which is in the land of Canaan, he and all the people who were with him. ⁷ And he built an altar there and called the place El Bethel, because there God appeared to him when he fled from the face of his brother.*

Likewise, the symbolic altars we raise for God in our lives also need to be constantly rebuilt and restored, by recommitting and rededicating ourselves to God, whenever we sense we have become lukewarm and complacent.

God renews his covenant with Jacob during this second encounter at Bethel because Jacob's season in distress had come to an end and God was moving him to his destiny. Jacob had been processed and he had been transformed sufficiently to qualify for a new name and identity.

Genesis 35:9-15 - Then God appeared to Jacob again, when he came from Padan Aram, and blessed him. 10 And God said to him, "Your name is Jacob; your name shall not be called Jacob anymore, but Israel shall be your name." So, He called his name Israel. 11 Also God said to him: "I am God Almighty. Be fruitful and multiply; a nation and a company of nations shall proceed from you, and kings shall come from your body. 12 The land which I gave Abraham and Isaac I give to you; and to your descendants after you I give this land." 13 Then God went up from him in the place where He talked with him. 14 So Jacob set up a pillar in the place where He talked with him, a pillar of stone; and he poured a drink offering on it, and he poured oil on it. 15 And Jacob called the name of the place where God spoke with him, Bethel.

When we begin to move from distress to destiny, we must also rebuild the broken altars of commitment in our lives and come up higher in our relationship with him, so he can also give us a new name for our new level. This second altar is stronger than the first because Jacob's trust and commitment to God had become stronger than it was during the first time and encounter. Likewise, our relationship with God must become stronger because it is the power in that relationship that will propel us to our place of promise and destiny.

As Jacob got ready to return to Bethel and enter his place of promise, there are three significant things he did that you must emulate as you return to your Bethel (your place of promise) and as God revisits His word over your life

Your "Rachel" Must Die

Genesis 35:16-18 - Then they journeyed from Bethel. And when there was but a little distance to go to Ephrath, Rachel labored in childbirth, and she had hard labor. [17] Now it came to pass, when she was in hard labor, that the midwife said to her, "Do not fear; you will have this son also." [18] And so it was, as her soul was departing (for she died), that she called his name Ben-Oni; but his father called him Benjamin.

Rachel was Jacob's favourite wife whose beauty had captivated Jacob and to some extent she had a strong hold on him. **Rachel** symbolizes vanity and your obsession with outward appearance and that which is carnal as opposed to that which is spiritual. Rachel represents covetousness and the cunning traits in us and our weaknesses for the idolatrous things despite being believers in the true God.

Rachel symbolizes that which you have obtained through hard labour and through your human efforts and self-help not by God's grace. Jacob had laboured hard for 14 years to win **Rachel's** hand in marriage. Often whatever we feel we have really laboured and fought for successfully, has a tendency to make us prideful and give us a sense of self-sufficiency. So, like Jacob all our "**Rachels**" must die **before** we enter our place of purpose and destiny.

You must bury your idols

(Genesis 35:2) And Jacob said to his household and to all who were *with him, "Put away the foreign gods that* are *among you, purify yourselves, and change your garments.*

This refers to things which control you and influence you away from destiny and God. You must burn your idols at Shechem, i.e., your material attachments and anything that seeks to replace your focus and worship of the true God. Sometimes while in the wilderness and in distress we may acquire certain toxic emotions and mindsets like bitterness, offense, pain and woundedness because of all that we have suffered. Such emotional baggage has no place at your place of promise and therefore you must release and let go of all that excess baggage.

Take back your authority, (Genesis 35:18)

And so it was, as her soul was departing (for she died), that she called his name Ben-Oni; but his father called him Benjamin

Rachel died birthing her last-born son and she named him **Ben-oni** a negative name i.e., *"son of my sorrow"*. Previously, Jacob had allowed his wives, Rachel and Leah to name his sons recklessly. Now as he returns to his place of promise he takes back his authority and names his son **Benjamin** which means *"son of my strength and son of my right hand."*

He in effect nullifies Rachel's negative naming thereby totally eliminating any negative idolatrous influence on Benjamin from Rachel. As you return to your Bethel, your place of promise, you must take authority over your life and your destiny and refuse to allow other people to label and define you and your promises erroneously.

Our moving from our place of distress to our place of destiny will involve a prophetic **promise**, a **ladder** experience, a **season** at Laban's, an **exit** from Laban's when that season is over, a **Peniel** experience, a **Shechem** lesson, a **confrontation** with our Esaus and finally a **return** to Bethel our place of promise and finally to Canaan our appointed destination.

As with Jacob, the prophetic promise and purpose over your life will move you from your distress to your destiny.

This Page Was Intentionally Left Blank

CHAPTER 4

The Power of Positioning

From The Cave To The Palace – The Story Of David

Chapter Preview

1. *Positioning Yourself in God's Promise*

2. *Positioning Yourself in the Move of God*

3. *Positioning Yourself in the Process*

4. *Positioning Yourself in the Corporate Vision First*

5. *Positioning Yourself for Transition and for Your Next Level*

6. *Positioning Yourself for Naming as a Mighty Man*

7. *Positioning Yourself in the Palace*

OPENING REMARKS

Moving from distress to Destiny entails moving from the "**cave**" (which symbolizes a place of insignificance, adversity where you are in hiding, isolation, rejection, persecution, without position or power, without resources, in debt, restlessness, in fear, separated from your loved ones and surrounded by others in distress like yourself) to the "**palace**" (which symbolizes a place of power and influence, honour, privileges and possessions, abundance etc.)

Positioning, basically means being located and settled and operating in the right place whether emotionally, mentally or physically for example in the right relationships, the right activities, the right choices and actions etc.

The story of David and his men who joined him in the wilderness while they were distressed debtors is a very powerful illustration of how to position yourself in order to move from distress to destiny.

1 Samuel 22:1-3 - David therefore departed from there and escaped to the cave of Adullam. So, when his brothers and all his father's house heard *it,* they went down there to him. ² And everyone *who was* in distress, everyone who *was* in debt, and everyone *who was* discontented gathered to him. So, he became captain over them. And there were about four hundred men with him. ³ Then David went from there to Mizpah of Moab; and he said to the king of Moab, "Please let my father and mother come here with you, till I know what God will do for me."

This story basically shows us how David and his distressed men underwent a process in the wilderness of making and moulding of character that transformed them from distressed, discontented debtors who were without identity or purpose into mighty men who now understood their true identity as David named them and they discovered their purpose towards fulfilling their destinies.

In this story of David and his mighty men discovered and understood several principles about right positioning that enabled them to make the full move from the cave to the palace, and if we emulate these positioning principles, we can also make our move from our place of distress to destiny effectively and successfully.

1. POSITIONING YOURSELF IN GOD'S PROMISE

Our move from distress to destiny will always begin with a promise and a prophetic word whereby God shows you His desired end for you, which is always a place of destiny.

God instructed his prophet Samuel to anoint David as the next king of Israel, which was quite a paradox because at that time Saul was still technically in office as king thereby making the promise to David sound inconceivable. Often, God will give us a promise that appears to be impossible because whatever He is calling us to lay hold of, is already in the possession of someone else, but we must receive God's word and promise by faith and believe that He knows how He will usher us into that promise.

1 Samuel 16:13-14 - Then Samuel took the horn of oil and anointed him in the midst of his brothers; and the Spirit of the Lord came upon David from that day forward. So, Samuel arose and went to Ramah. ¹⁴ But the Spirit of the Lord departed from Saul, and a distressing spirit from the Lord troubled him.

In addition, after being anointed, David returns to tend the sheep in the wilderness as opposed to being installed on the throne as king and perhaps this is the most puzzling thing because David spent the next 25 years or so, struggling to survive in the wilderness in distress with other distressed people. It is understandable how David and even those around him may have reached a point where they doubted the promise and the word of God to David.

This goes to show us that it will take time for God to move us from the promise to the palace and again we must trust His timing.

We learn several things here;

a) Your promise will come years before you possess it. David was anointed to be king of Israel and given the prophetic promise, years before he eventually sat on the throne at Hebron, as king. The prophetic word over your life will be tested and tried in the wilderness and it will take every ounce of faith in you to hold on to it.

b) Your brethren will witness ("in the midst of his brethren") you being given the prophetic word and promise and they may mock and taunt you when it takes too long to manifest and be fulfilled.

c) Like David, you may be a nobody and perhaps the least either in your family, church, workplace or organization, society etc. when God decides to give you a prophetic promise and word. In other words, you have been overlooked, hidden and underestimated, yet God has been preparing you as you continued to serve Him faithfully in some insignificant position and place which your brethren consider irrelevant.

They erroneously assume that the reason you are serving in that insignificant place is because you are not worthy and not good enough to serve in the "King's army" (which symbolizes the more important assignments). Yet remember that God's hand is upon you and He is deliberately hiding you and the greatness within you from your enemies as He makes and matures you for greater things.

1 Samuel 17:28 - *Now Eliab his oldest brother heard when he spoke to the men; and Eliab's anger was aroused against David,* *and he said, "Why did you come down here? And with whom have you left those few sheep in the wilderness? I know your pride and the insolence of your heart, for you have come down to see the battle."*

d) You will be found in God's presence-worshipping and ministering to God's sheep symbolizing God's people, rearing and nurturing them because like David you have a heart for God's sheep and that is why you are a man after God's own heart.

1 Samuel 16:11 - And Samuel said to Jesse, "Are all the young men here?" Then he said, "There remains yet the youngest, and there he is, keeping the sheep." And Samuel said to Jesse, "Send and bring him. For we will not sit down till he comes here."

e) No one saw you kill the bear and the lion so your gifting, skills and anointing is still hidden and that's why the prophetic promise sounds ridiculous to your brethren.

1 Samuel 17:34-35 - But David said to Saul, "Your servant used to keep his father's sheep, and when a lion or a bear came and took a lamb out of the flock, 35 I went out after it and struck it, and delivered the lamb from its mouth; and when it arose against me, I caught it by its beard, and struck and killed it.

f) When he killed Goliath, it was his first major victory in public using one stone called faith in God. This happens in the presence of his brethren who had underestimated him and dismissed him as a nobody.

1 Samuel 17:49 - Then David put his hand in his bag and took out a stone; and he slung it and struck the Philistine in his forehead, so that the stone sank into his forehead, and he fell on his face to the earth.

g) The other four stones were used to kill four other giants by David's men many years later, symbolizing the power of teamwork and corporate anointing, because in time you will be raised by your Set man as a mighty man to help your Set man to kill and slay all other giants standing in the way of your Set man's destiny and your own destiny.

2 Samuel 21:22 - These four were born to the giant in Gath, and fell by the hand of David and by the hand of his servants.

h) Your first major victory in public (killing Goliath) is not a sign that you have "arrived" or reached. The journey has just began and the process of your making and moulding has just began, so you must not develop a prideful attitude and spirit because you have a long way to go and many more major battles to fight before you eventually reach your palace.

2. POSITIONING YOURSELF IN THE NEW MOVE OF GOD

A "**Move of God**" is a fresh supernatural, spiritual, power, awakening, revival orchestrated by God among a people, a church community or a Nation, which is usually accompanied by signs wonders, and a mighty presence of God.

It is when the spirit of God moves mightily to compel a shift, transformation, reform in order to carry out His agenda, especially to draw people to Himself.

The first move of God is found in *Genesis 1:1-2*

In the beginning God created the heavens and the earth. The earth was without form, and void; and darkness was on the face of the deep. And the Spirit of God was hovering over the face of the waters.

Some of the other great moves of God in the bible are for example; during the time of **Moses**, when God was delivering his children from Egypt, during **Noah's** time when God was grieved by the wickedness of the people also during the time of **Elijah** when God was distinguishing between Baal and true worship, also during **Elisha** when God was demonstrating His miraculous power, and during the time of **Jesus** when God was redeeming mankind. In the Body of Christ, the Welsh Revival (1904-1905), the Azusa Street 1906-1915 and the Tukutendeza Yesu, the Bakole Revival in East Africa 1931-1936 are notable Moves of God.

Every Move of God has its carriers, supporters, preservers, sustainers as well as its defilers, opposers, persecutors and killers. Suffice to say, a Move of God usually entails judgment as God moves to establish His righteousness and holiness.

God was establishing a new order in Israel because Saul had disobeyed, so God rejected him and chose David to replace him.

Saul purported to operate in the wrong office and in the wrong anointing when he made sacrifices, as he got impatient waiting for Samuel. In doing so, Saul disobeyed God by stepping out of his anointing as **king** and seeking to operate in the anointing and office of a **priest** and thereby breaching and undermining the divine order of God as regards the distinct offices and anointings of priest and king.

1 Samuel 13:8-9 - Then he waited seven days, according to the time set by Samuel. But Samuel did not come to Gilgal; and the people were scattered from him. ⁹ So Saul said, "Bring a burnt offering and peace offerings here to me." And he offered the burnt offering.

God termed Saul's disobedience as the sin of witchcraft and reminded us that obedience is always better than sacrifice. Saul feared the people more than God, and his disobedience to God was an attempt to please men, because he valued the opinion of men more than he valued the opinion of God.

1 Samuel 13:11-12 - And Samuel said, "What have you done?" Saul said, "When I saw that the people were scattered from me, and that you did not come within the days appointed, and that the Philistines gathered together at Michmash, ¹² then I said, 'The Philistines will now come down on me at Gilgal, and I have not made supplication to the Lord.' Therefore, I felt compelled, and offered a burnt offering."

God also rejected Saul when he disobeyed God's strict instructions to kill and destroy all the Amalekites but instead Saul decided to save some.

1 Samuel 15:18-19 - Now the Lord sent you on a mission, and said, 'Go, and utterly destroy the sinners, the Amalekites, and fight against them until they are consumed.' ¹⁹ Why then did you not obey the voice of the Lord? Why did you swoop down on the spoil, and do evil in the sight of the Lord?"

As we move from distress to destiny, we must be careful that we do not disobey God by operating in the wrong office or anointing because this is a breach of God's order. When we haven't discovered our true calling and purpose then chances are we will seek to operate in a calling and purpose that is not ours and in so doing we end up sinning against God.

1 Samuel 13:13 - And Samuel said to Saul, "You have done foolishly. You have not kept the commandment of the Lord your God, which He commanded you. For now the Lord would have established your kingdom over Israel forever.

In David, God found the qualities that pleased Him.

i. A man after God's own heart – a true worshipper

> **1 Samuel 13:14 - But now your kingdom shall not continue. The Lord has sought for Himself a man after His own heart, and the Lord has commanded him *to be* commander over His people, because you have not kept what the Lord commanded you."**

Total obedience to God is crucial in our journey to destiny.

ii. A man who constantly enquired from God – a reliance on God not self and he walked wisely. We find several scriptures where David enquired of the Lord (**1 Samuel 38:8, 1 Samuel 23:2, 2 Samuel 5:19, 2 Samuel 2:1, 2 Samuel 21:1, 2 Samuel 3:1-6, 1 Samuel 18:12-14**)

> **1 Samuel 18:14 - And David behaved wisely in all his ways, and the Lord *was* with him.**

Like David, we must constantly enquire of God and seek His wisdom and directions in order to move from distress to destiny.

iii. A man who understood the power and value of spiritual authority and divine order e.g. he respected and honoured, Samuel the prophet of God. David constantly went back to Samuel for spiritual empowerment and guidance.

iv. A man who respected and honoured the office of the priest so he respected those in the priesthood like Abiathar (Son of Abimelech) with the ephod that was used to enquire of God. David also respected and honoured the office of the Prophets like Samuel and Nathan and sought their wise counsel.

God was doing a new thing, a new beginning a revival and an establishing of His will, plan and purposes which birthed a powerful new move. The "**David generation**" was emerging to establish the purposes of God in Israel to be a people were after God's own heart, worshippers of God, enquirers of God like David and who would have an understanding and respect for the different offices and anointings of the prophet, priest and King.

Our **spiritual positioning** determines our destiny, so you must identify and align yourself with what God is doing. In this story we see how David's men positioned themselves in the new move of God;

- The distressed-discontented debtors discerned that David was God's anointed and chosen one and they connected and submitted under him. David had nothing, Saul had all the vineyards, meaning he had all the resources to maintain a mighty army. David was God's chosen and he was the new move and the new dispensation and even though David had no material substance to give these men, yet they knew that God's hand and favor was upon David, so provision would eventually come.

  1 Samuel 22:7 - then Saul said to his servants who stood about him, "Hear now, you Benjamites! Will the son of Jesse give every one of you fields and vineyards, and make you all captains of thousands and captains of hundreds?

- The distressed discontented men realized that God had rejected the old guard in Israel (Saul) and they chose the new guard (David) through whom they would enter their Destiny.

- Jonathan (Saul's son) also realized that David was the new move of God that had replaced his father but unfortunately although he helped David, he still chose to remain under his father Saul (the old move) instead of positioning himself with David (the new move). (Jonathan probably preferred the comforts of the palace and he was not ready for the harshness of the wilderness).

When God begins to move us from distress to destiny, we will have to make radical destiny choices and some of these choices will include settling for what is comfortable and convenient or choosing the hard but right path to our destiny.

1 Samuel 23:16-18 - Then Jonathan, Saul's son, arose and went to David in the woods and strengthened his hand in God. ¹⁷ And he said to him, "Do not fear, for the hand of Saul my father shall not find you. You shall be king over Israel, and I shall be next to you. Even my father Saul knows that." ¹⁸ So the two of them made a covenant before the Lord. And David stayed in the woods, and Jonathan went to his own house.

- The men of David soon realized that connecting with David, the new move of God, came at a high price and cost, but they also knew that it would be worth it in the end.

Sometimes we may not recognize a new move of God, because it will not be where we expect it to be. The men of David positioned themselves in the new move of God at that time which was in the cave.

Supporting the move of God (which represents the purposes and plans of God at any particular time and dispensation or at a particular place or for a particular people) will cost you dearly because there will always be enemies of the move of God who are constantly seeking to destroy and kill that new move of God (especially those representing the old move and old guard otherwise known as the old priesthood).

When God rejects an old guard, they embark on fighting the new move of God. Every new move of God is usually birthed through one person or one group who God anoints to carry that move and God also assigns a people to connect to that person or group and help fulfil God's purposes within that new move. Moses, David, Elijah, Elisha, Noah, Joshua, the Apostles etc. are some of the servants, God used to carry his moves.

So, in this case David was the one anointed to carry the new move and anyone who supported and helped him was constantly in danger from Saul (the old move). The household of priests at Nob assisted David when he was running away from Saul and gave him bread and the sword which symbolized that they fed, empowered and equipped him as he continued to escape from Saul.

1 Samuel 21:6-9 - So the priest gave him holy bread; for there was no bread there but the showbread which had been taken from before the Lord, in order to put hot bread in its place on the day when it was taken away. ⁷ Now a certain man of the servants of Saul was there that day, detained before the Lord. And his name was Doeg, an Edomite, the chief of the herdsmen who belonged to Saul. ⁸ And David said to Ahimelech, "Is there not here on hand a spear or a sword? For I have brought neither my sword nor my weapons with me, because the king's business required haste." ⁹ So the priest said, "The sword of Goliath the Philistine, whom you killed in the Valley of Elah, there it is, wrapped in a cloth behind the ephod. If you will take that, take it. For there is no other except that one here." And David said, "There is none like it; give it to me."

The old move and old guard will always play victim in an attempt to discredit you and smear your reputation and defame your character and this is what Saul did when he got to the household of priests at Nob.

1 Samuel 22:13 - Then Saul said to him, "Why have you conspired against me, you and the son of Jesse, in that you have given him bread and a sword, and have inquired of God for him, that he should rise against me, to lie in wait, as it is this day?"

Fortunately, the priests had a revelation that David was God's chosen and they had to stand with him in order for the purposes of God to be fulfilled.

In our moving from distress to destiny, another crucial destiny decision we will have to make is in discerning what God is doing at any particular time, distinguishing between God's move and the moves of the enemy or the moves of man's flesh and carnality. The priests were killed by Saul for supporting and positioning themselves in the new move of God, namely David

1 Samuel 22:16-19 – ⁱ⁶ And the king said, "You shall surely die, Ahimelech, you and all your father's house!" ¹⁷ Then the king said to the guards who stood about him, "Turn and kill the priests of the Lord, because their hand also is with David, and because they knew when he fled and did not tell it to me." But the servants of the king would not lift their hands to strike the priests of the Lord. ¹⁸ And the king said to Doeg, "You turn and kill the priests!" So, Doeg the Edomite turned and struck the priests, and killed on that day eighty-five men who wore a linen ephod. ¹⁹ Also Nob, the city of the priests, he struck with the edge of the sword, both men and women, children and nursing infants, oxen and donkeys and sheep—with the edge of the sword.

Beware of the spirit of "**Doeg and Edomite**" which symbolizes persecution and seeks to kill all who are loyal to the new move including those who feed and equip the set man who carries that move.

The price you pay for positioning yourself in the move of God and supporting the move of God is never in vain because out of your loyalty and faithfulness to that move arises a "**covenant of protection**". In other words, as long as you are positioned in God's plan and purposes there is always a canopy of grace and protection. Even when the old move and old guard persecute and kill the new move and new guard, there is always a remnant that God preserves for Himself.

In this passage we find that Abiathar escaped from being killed at Nob and he ran to David and David assured him of a "**covenant of protection**".

1 Samuel 22:20-23 *Now one of the sons of Ahimelech the son of Ahitub, named Abiathar, escaped and fled after David. And Abiathar told David that Saul had killed the Lord's priests. So, David said to Abiathar, "I knew that day, when Doeg the Edomite was there, that he would surely tell Saul. I have caused the death of all the persons of your father's house. Stay with me; do not fear. For he who seeks my life seeks your life, but with me you shall be safe."*

It is interesting to note that the men of David now had **swords** (symbolizing word of God) whereas at the beginning they didn't have any.

1 Samuel 25:13 - Then David said to his men, "Every man gird on his sword." So, every man girded on his sword, and David also girded on his sword. And about four hundred men went with David, and two hundred stayed with the supplies.

This means that over time after connecting with David they became equipped and empowered. Your Set man has a mandate to feed you with the word of God and after every battle you win in the spirit you will grow in your knowledge and ability to divide the word of God rightly. Likewise, every battle David and his men won they acquired swords and other weapons which made them even more effective in battle and increased their skills.

Your ability to successfully move from your distress to your destiny will be determined by the relationships you choose to connect yourself with and in particular your relationship with your Set man of God who is also your spiritual authority and spiritual midwife and who has a mandate to nurture, equip and usher you to destiny. That authority must be able to hear God as he leads you and others, otherwise you will remain in distress.

There are **two key things** that demonstrate that David was a leader who heard God and therefore the kind of leader we ought to follow;

a) **Firstly,** David chose to win by righteousness and refused to touch the anointed of God despite his men urging him to. David's character had already been formed, so he refused to follow wrong (emotional) advice from his men and he refused to kill Saul. (1ˢᵗ Sam 24:4) **"Then the men of David said to him, "*This is the day of which the Lord said to you, 'Behold, I will deliver your enemy into your hand, that you may do to him as it seems good to you.'" And David arose and secretly cut off a corner of Saul's robe."***

David was so remorseful for cutting a piece of Saul's robe, showing how sensitive he was in the spirit, and how easily convicted he was of any wrong doing because he was a man after God's own heart. Anytime we seek to take matters into our own hands in order to expedite our moving from distress to destiny (instead of trusting God and walking in righteousness) we will stumble and jeopardize our journey to destiny

This was a major test for David because Saul was the only obstacle between the wilderness and the palace and David could have expedited his entry to the throne at Hebron by killing Saul but he decided to trust and wait on God's timing instead of taking matters in his own hands. Like David we must choose to win through righteousness and in God's timing.

b) **Secondly,** a wise leader is flexible where need arises and he is always ready to change his mind where circumstances and wisdom warrant it. So, when David encountered foolish Nabal and he could have killed him, he nonetheless changed his mind when Abigail prevailed upon him and he saw her reasoning.

(**1st Sam 25:23-26**) *Now when Abigail saw David, she dismounted quickly from the donkey, fell on her face before David, and bowed down to the ground. 24 So she fell at his feet and said: "On me, my lord, on me let this iniquity be! And please let your maidservant speak in your ears, and hear the words of your maidservant. 25 Please, let not my lord regard this scoundrel Nabal. For as his name is, so is he: Nabal is his name, and folly is with him! But I, your maidservant, did not see the young men of my lord whom you sent. 26 Now therefore, my lord, as the Lord lives and as your soul lives, since the Lord has held you back from coming to bloodshed and from avenging yourself with your own hand, now then, let your enemies and those who seek harm for my lord be as Nabal.*

David therefore restrained himself from acting emotionally in anger and he refused to allow Nabal's foolishness to derail his focus on where God was taking him.

3. POSITIONING YOURSELF IN THE PROCESS

Between the **promise** and the **palace**, you will undergo the **process** of your making and moulding in order to mature you and refine your character for the palace and the greater responsibilities there. This means that the magnitude and weight of the promises God has given you and that He is ushering you into, is so great, that unless you have embraced the process of your making and allowed God to lay strong foundations within you, you will not be able to handle those promises and the greatness that comes with them.

Once God had chosen David, He embarked on a rigorous training regime. The Psalms are full of David's distress he endured, and the tears he shed but it was during those times that God developed him into one of the greatest Kings Israel would have.

 a) Dealing with Betrayal (1 Samuel 23:1-14)

One of the aspects of the process that David and his men had to endure is dealing with betrayal especially for those you have helped and sacrificed for.

(1 Samuel 23:12-13) Then David said, "Will the men of Keilah deliver me and my men into the hand of Saul?" And the Lord said, "They will deliver you." [13] *So David and his men, about six hundred, arose and departed from Keilah and went wherever they could go. Then it was told Saul that David had escaped from Keilah; so, he halted the expedition.*

Keilah was Saul's jurisdiction so David was locked in a dangerous place of betrayal but God gave David an escape and a way out. Your response and reaction to betrayal can make you or break you so you must purpose to obey God without expecting gratitude from people you have helped and protected.

Betrayal is part of the process you must undergo and endure as you move from the cave to the palace, so you must learn to manage your expectations from people, and keep your eyes and focus on the palace without allowing the chains of betrayal to hold you back.

After the painful experience at Keilah the distressed men following David increased from 400 to 600 meaning that David's mature response to betrayal testified to and encouraged many more to join David in their journey to Destiny. Your pain often becomes a power that propels others to their Destiny, when you respond to that pain properly.

David had enquired of the Lord and had already known that the people of Keilah would betray him, this means that when we walk closely with God in our journey from distress to destiny, He will reveal things to us that will help us manage our expectations and guard our hearts from failing and to guide us to be prepared and equipped for every adversity.

b) Dealing with false accusations and slander

Being slandered and defamed is another part of the process that we will need to endure as we move from distress to destiny and to ensure that we do not allow the pain and humiliation of slander and deformation to keep us bound in bitterness and offense that will either delay or prevent us from moving on. Saul kept slandering David, but David never slandered Saul back.

(1 Samuel 22:7-8) *then Saul said to his servants who stood about him, "Hear now, you Benjamites! Will the son of Jesse give every one of you fields and vineyards, and make you all captains of thousands and captains of hundreds? ⁸ All of you have conspired against me, and there is no one who reveals to me that my son has made a covenant with the son of Jesse; and there is not one of you who is sorry for me or reveals to me that my son has stirred up my servant against me, to lie in wait, as it is this day."*

In the end Saul cursed himself and blessed David

(1ˢᵗ Sam 26:25) *"Then Saul said to David, "May you be blessed, my son David! You shall both do great things and also still prevail. So, David went on his way, and Saul returned to his place."*

When he became convicted by David's decision to walk in righteousness and when he saw David refused to sin against God by touching the anointed of God. Saul saw his own wickedness and testified of David's righteousness. Let your enemy testify about you, don't justify yourself let God vindicate you like he vindicated David. Our ability to persevere and endure patiently through false accusations and slanders is part of the process of our making and moulding.

c) Dealing with offenses and snares

The word of God in Proverbs says offenses will come and if we are not careful to let go of those offenses, they will ensnare us into losing focus as to where we are headed (namely to our destiny from our distress). David's enemy (Saul) had no free gifts and every gift had strings attached with a hidden agenda and motive, so when he gave his daughter Michal to David as a prize, it was with an ulterior motive. Saul's daughter Michal was to be a snare to David.

(1st Sam.18:21) *"So Saul said, "I will give her to him, that she may be a snare to him, and that the hand of the Philistines may be against him." Therefore, Saul said to David a second time, "You shall be my son-in-law today."*

So, David stayed away from Michal until he had passed the danger zone, because he was alert to of Saul's devices. The Old priesthood and old guard will entice you with material gifts, when they realize that you are God's new move, that is replacing them. This may happen in your workplace and organization or in any other situation where God is lifting you up to take up positions where you will fulfil his purposes because those who He had placed there have disobeyed Him and He has rejected them.

d) Dealing with manipulative spirits

There was a young man who came to David carrying Saul's crown after Saul had been wounded in battle. He confessed that he had found Saul wounded and he actually indulged Saul's request to kill him because Saul did not want to die by the hand of the enemy. This man thought that David would rejoice and reward him and perhaps that David would be indebted to him for life, but David swiftly ordered the execution of this man for having dared to kill the anointed of God, Saul.

2 Samuel 1:6-10; 14-16 - Then the young man who told him said, "As I happened by chance to be on Mount Gilboa, there was Saul, leaning on his spear; and indeed, the chariots and horsemen followed hard after him. ⁷ Now when he looked behind him, he saw me and called to me. And I answered, 'Here I am.' ⁸ And he said to me, 'Who are you?' So, I answered him, 'I am an Amalekite.' ⁹ He said to me again, 'Please stand over me and kill me, for anguish has come upon me, but my life still remains in me.' ¹⁰ So I stood over him and killed him, because I was sure that he could not live after he had fallen. And I took the crown that was on his head and the bracelet that was on his arm, and have brought them here to my lord."

¹⁴ So David said to him, "How was it you were not afraid to put forth your hand to destroy the Lord's anointed?" ¹⁵ Then David called one of the young men and said, "Go near, and execute him!" And he struck him so that he died. ¹⁶ So David said to him, "Your blood is on your own head, for your own mouth has testified against you, saying, 'I have killed the Lord's anointed."

God alone must get the glory for your success, so always beware of those who didn't walk your walk nor suffer with you in the wilderness but who now seek to join you after the battle. Their intention is to take credit for what God has done through you and to selfishly ride on your victory whereas they were not prepared to stand with you when you were in the valley.

In addition, there will also be those who God may use to help you to move from your distress to destiny but who may later try to manipulate and control you on the grounds that you owe them.

If you give in to this kind of blackmail you will end up living in fear and maybe even depositioning yourself from the plans and purposes of God as you try to indulge the unreasonable demands of such people.

e) Escaping the spear of Saul

1 Samuel 18:11 - And Saul cast the spear, for he said, "I will pin David to the wall!" But David escaped his presence twice.

1 Samuel 19:10 - Then Saul sought to pin David to the wall with the spear, but he slipped away from Saul's presence; and he drove the spear into the wall. So, David fled and escaped that night.

Perhaps one of the most difficult challenges David had to endure as part of the process was escaping the "**spear of Saul**". The spear of Saul comes when you least expect it, when your enemy has lured you into a place of false security.

The "**spear of Saul**" represents the vicious attacks by the rejected old guard and old move or priesthood who will constantly seek to spear and kill the new move of God, and pin him against the wall (meaning to silence and paralyze him from reaching his place of promise and fulfilling the plans of God). Beware of the "**spears of Saul**" that may seek to pin you down in your family, your church, your workplace, at your sphere and place of assignment

f) Dealing with in-house opposition

Your process in the wilderness will also entail handling in in-house opposition and internal uprising which is usually worse than external opposition and external uprising. When David and his men got to Ziklag, they faced one of their greatest challenges just on the eve of their breakthrough and their entry into the palace.

Often our greatest testing will come just before we step into our promises and it will take a lot of spiritual discernment to understand the enemy's attempt to hinder us at the last moment when we have already come so far, fought so hard and suffered so much.

(**1ˢᵗ Sam 30: 1-3** - *Now it happened, when David and his men came to Ziklag, on the third day, that the Amalekites had invaded the South and Ziklag, attacked Ziklag and burned it with fire, ² and had taken captive the women and those who were there, from small to great; they did not kill anyone, but carried them away and went their way. ³ So David and his men came to the city, and there it was, burned with fire; and their wives, their sons, and their daughters had been taken captive.*

David and his men were stripped of everything that they had gained so far and we can understand their devastation and frustration because it seemed like everything, they had worked so hard for, had now been taken away by the enemy.

It may often happen in our own journey from distress to destiny that we reach a place where we encounter such devastating losses (whether in terms of our loved ones, relationships, positions and possessions) and this may paralyze us from arising and finishing the few remaining steps into our promises.

At this point David's men lost focus and they even lost trust in their Set man David, who they now wanted to stone. The corporate team spirit that had been their greatest strength at the cave and in the wilderness was being tested.

1ˢᵗ Sam 30: 4-6 *Then David and the people who were with him lifted up their voices and wept, until they had no more power to weep. And David's two wives, Ahinoam the Jezreelitess, and Abigail the widow of Nabal the Carmelite, had been taken captive. Now David was greatly distressed, for the people spoke of stoning him, because the soul of all the people was grieved, every man for his sons and his daughters. But David strengthened himself in the Lord his God.*

Fortunately, after his initial shock, David arose to take charge over the situation, because he had matured as a leader through the wilderness and he knew that the key in restoring the strength of his men was by being strong himself and offering leadership at this critical point.

1ˢᵗ **Sam 30: 7-8**

Then David said to Abiathar the priest, Ahimelech's son, "Please bring the ephod here to me." And Abiathar brought the ephod to David. So, David inquired of the Lord, saying, "Shall I pursue this troop? Shall I overtake them?"

And He answered him, "Pursue, for you shall surely overtake them and without fail recover all."

God is faithful and he will never leave us or forsake us and, in this passage, we see the victory He gives David and his men.

1ˢᵗ **Sam 30:17-20**

Then David attacked them from twilight until the evening of the next day. Not a man of them escaped, except four hundred young men who rode on camels and fled. So, David recovered all that the Amalekites had carried away, and David rescued his two wives.

And nothing of theirs was lacking, either small or great, sons or daughters, spoil or anything which they had taken from them; David recovered all. Then David took all the flocks and herds they had driven before those other livestock, and said, "This is David's spoil."

g) Dealing with the welfare of all

The process in the wilderness had indeed built character in David and this is evidenced by the principle he established after the recovery at Ziklag when he said that from henceforth those who fought and those who stayed behind would share the spoils of war alike.

David was recognizing that there are those who may fight with you physically in the battlefield and there are those who may remain behind to pray and intercede and others who will stay behind and watch the spoils and that each therefore plays a role that must be rewarded.

This principle had the effect of greatly cementing the unity in David's army, and it also demonstrated that there is no room for selfishness in the journey from distress to destiny.

1st Sam 30:21-25

[21] Now David came to the two hundred men who had been so weary that they could not follow David, whom they also had made to stay at the Brook Besor. So, they went out to meet David and to meet the people who were with him. And when David came near the people, he greeted them. [22] Then all the wicked and worthless men of those who went with David answered and said, "Because they did not go with us, we will not give them any of the spoil that we have recovered, except for every man's wife and children, that they may lead them away and depart." [23] But David said, "My brethren, you

shall not do so with what the Lord has given us, who has preserved us and delivered into our hand the troop that came against us. [24] For who will heed you in this matter? But as his part is who goes down to the battle, so shall his part be who stays by the supplies; they shall share alike." [25] So it was, from that day forward; he made it a statute and an ordinance for Israel to this day.

h) Hiding your greatness in divine foolishness

Part of the process of your making and moulding in the wilderness as you move from distress to destiny will entail learning how to escape from your enemies by hiding your greatness within divine foolishness. As long as your enemies consider you as irrelevant, they will not see you as a threat and hence they will not fight you which gives you space to do what God has called you to do.

(1 Samuel 21:10-15) Then David arose and fled that day from before Saul, and went to Achish the king of Gath. [11] And the servants of Achish said to him, "Is this not David the king of the land? Did they not sing of him to one another in dances, saying: 'Saul has slain his thousands, And David his ten thousands'?" [12] Now David took these words to heart, and was very much afraid of Achish the king of Gath. [13] So he changed his behavior before them, pretended madness in their hands, scratched on the doors of the gate, and let his saliva fall down on his beard. [14] Then Achish said to his servants, "Look, you see the man is insane. Why have you brought him to me? [15] Have I need of madmen, that you have brought this fellow to play the madman in my presence? Shall this fellow come into my house?"

i) Embracing your threshing, purging and pruning

The process between the cave and the palace will also entail threshing, purging and pruning as your character is moulded to mature you for the palace. The men of David had matured through submission and obedience to David their Set man. David had also matured and chosen to win through righteousness not by carnal means: -

1 Samuel 24:4-7 Then the men of David said to him, "This is the day of which the Lord said to you, 'Behold, I will deliver your enemy into your hand, that you may do to him as it seems good to you." And David arose and secretly cut off a corner of Saul's robe. ⁵ Now it happened afterward that David's heart troubled him because he had cut Saul's robe. ⁶ And he said to his men, "The Lord forbid that I should do this thing to my master, the Lord's anointed, to stretch out my hand against him, seeing he is the anointed of the Lord." ⁷ So David restrained his servants with these words, and did not allow them to rise against Saul. And Saul got up from the cave and went on his way.

As you move from distress to destiny you must guard against being led by your carnality and flesh and instead be led by the Holy Spirit so that you do not miss your purpose and destiny.

Even though David himself had matured in character and he had a clear understanding that his victory would come by trusting and waiting on God, nonetheless, not all his men had matured to that level. So, David had to restrain them from becoming impatient and resulting to carnal means by killing Saul the anointed of God.

David instructed his men, to let God fight for them. Fortunately, his men had learnt obedience and to trust David so even though they may not have understood why they should not kill Saul and expedite their entering into the palace, they chose to listen to David.

j)   **Distinguishing between Corporate and Personal testing**

David and his men had been severely tested as a group and team throughout in the wilderness and they had come to understand

and accept that this kind of "**corporate testing**" meant taking responsibility collectively, incurring liabilities and losses jointly would eventually lead to corporate benefits.

(1 Chronicles 11:1-3) - Then all Israel came together to David at Hebron, saying, "Indeed we are your bone and your flesh. ² Also, in time past, even when Saul was king, you were the one who led Israel out and brought them in; and the Lord your God said to you, 'You shall shepherd My people Israel, and be ruler over My people Israel.' ³ Therefore all the elders of Israel came to the king at Hebron, and David made a covenant with them at Hebron before the Lord. And they anointed David king over Israel, according to the word of the Lord by Samuel.

David was eventually crowned king over all of Israel according to the prophetic promise that Samuel had given him many years before, and he finally sat on the throne at Hebron but there was only one crown and only one throne, so the next question was what would happen to his men who had faithfully followed him from the cave through the wilderness right up to where he had now reached.

Corporately, the purpose of God had been achieved and David and his distressed men had undergone "**corporate**" testing (or testing as a team), and they had passed the tests by embracing the process of their making.

So now it became personal and each man had to undergo a "**personal testing**" to also enter their own part of the palace and fulfil their own part of their destiny. As you push your Set man to his next level it means that you will also enter your next level because the divine covenant relationship benefits both of you.

The corporate vision and purpose of the Set man had been fulfilled by David entering Hebron and sitting as King over Judah (and later as king over Israel) in accordance with the word of God through

Prophet Samuel. This corporate vision and purpose had been established through **corporate testing** i.e., the men had been taken through tests as a team **collectively** which they passed as a team collectively and corporately, because they all related to set man "**as a group**" (a corporate unit).

However, now for the next level they were entering the palace and for the kind of service they would be required to render to the set man, the men needed to relate to their set man "**on a one on one**", so that their hearts towards set man could be tested. This next level of "success" would require a higher level of service and loyalty and submission.

Unlike in the wilderness where they owned nothing and so they did not have much to lose, but at Hebron there was much to lose because much was entrusted to them in terms of resources and the lives of all the people their set man David would rule over.

To whom much is given much is required, the standard of obedience and commitment rises depending on measures of responsibility, so your service to set men when he has entered his promised land, becomes more crucial and demanding. The test of loyalty is higher and stricter and it's personal not a group thing. i.e. are you willing to stand with the set man even if you are left alone (not as a group)?

Now the time had come for David to name his men and give them positions because circumcision needed to come before they could be named by their set man and spiritual father.

David had been their captain so once he became king there was a vacancy for that position of the captain of the army and while David could have assigned it to any one of them especially to his cousin Joab, he decided to give every man a fair chance to vie and qualify for that position. So, David gave them the first test.

Test 1: To Kill The Jebusites (The Lame, Blind)

Joab swiftly destroyed the Jebusites and he legitimately qualified to become captain of the army.

2 Samuel 5:6 - And the king and his men went to Jerusalem against the Jebusites, the inhabitants of the land, who spoke to David, saying, "You shall not come in here; but the blind and the lame will repel you," thinking, "David cannot come in here."

These Jebusites were a potential threat to hindering David from entering Jerusalem (Centre of Power). The Jebusites symbolise those hindrances seeking to hinder your set man from possessing his full promises-full package and full manifestation. You must "Kill" through prayer/intercession/word of authority all such Jebusites.

1 Chronicles 11:4-6 - And David and all Israel went to Jerusalem, which is Jebus, where the Jebusites were, the inhabitants of the land. ⁵ But the inhabitants of Jebus said to David, "You shall not come in here!" Nevertheless, David took the stronghold of Zion (that is, the City of David). ⁶ Now David said, "Whoever attacks the Jebusites first shall be chief and captain." And Joab the son of Zeruiah went up first, and became chief.

The second test, David gave his men was;

Test 2: To Get Water From Well Of Bethlehem

2 Samuel 23:15-17 - And David said with longing, "Oh, that someone would give me a drink of the water from the well of Bethlehem, which is by the gate!" ¹⁶ So the three mighty men broke through the camp of the Philistines, drew water from the well of Bethlehem that was by the gate, and took it and brought it to David. Nevertheless, he would not drink it, but poured it out to the Lord. ¹⁷ And he said, "Far be it from me, O Lord, that I should do this! Is this not the blood of the men who went in jeopardy of their lives?" Therefore, he would not drink it.

This story about bravery and loyalty is repeated in;

1 Chronicles 11:17-19 - And David said with longing, "Oh, that someone would give me a drink of water from the well of Bethlehem, which is by the gate!" [18] So the three broke through the camp of the Philistines, drew water from the well of Bethlehem that *was* by the gate, and took *it* and brought *it* to David. Nevertheless, David would not drink it, but poured it out to the Lord. [19] And he said, "Far be it from me, O my God, that I should do this! Shall I drink the blood of these men *who have put* their lives *in jeopardy?* For at the risk of their lives they brought it." Therefore, he would not drink it. These things were done by the three mighty men.

To get a cup of water from the well of Bethlehem through the garrison of the Philistines to quench the set man, three men did it and they became mighty men of David. Moving from distress to Destiny entails; **naming** after circumcision and testing and positioning in the Kingdom

The Third testing came later and progressively;

Test 3: To Slay The Remaining 4 Giants

David had already killed the first giant Goliath and we are told that he only used one smooth stone out of the 5 smooth stones he had, so the remaining 4 stones were for his men to use in order to kill the 4 remaining giants.

A Giant symbolises all those things hindering you and your set man entering and possessing your promised land.

So there remained 4 giants who were later slain by David's men as they became positioned in protecting David (the Lamp of Israel).

One giant was slain by Abishai, another one was slain by Sibbechi, another one by Elhanan and the last giant was slain by Jonathan, David's brother and hence each of these men qualified for positions in the palace as mighty men for passing this test of slaying the giants.

(2 Sam.21:15-22 *"When the Philistines were at war again with Israel, David and his servants with him went down and fought against the Philistines; and David grew faint. [16] Then Ishbi-Benob, who was one of the sons of [a] the giant, the weight of whose bronze spear was three hundred shekels, who was bearing a new sword, thought he could kill David. [17] But Abishai the son of Zeruiah came to his aid, and struck the Philistine and killed him. Then the men of David swore to him, saying, "You shall go out no more with us to battle, lest you quench the lamp of Israel."[18] Now it happened afterward that there was again a battle with the Philistines at Gob. Then Sibbechai the Hushathite killed Saph, who was one of the sons of the giant. [19] Again there was war at Gob with the Philistines, where Elhanan the son of Jaare-Oregim the Bethlehemite killed the brother of Goliath the Gittite, the shaft of whose spear was like a weaver's beam. [20] Yet again there was war at Gath, where there was a man of great stature, who had six fingers on each hand and six toes on each foot, twenty-four in number; and he also was born to the giant. [21] So when he defied Israel, Jonathan the son of Shimea, David's brother, killed him. [22] These four were born to the giant in Gath, and fell by the hand of David and by the hand of his servants."*)

Moving from distress to destiny will require us to pass these 3 tests namely, overcoming everything that seeks to hinder our Set man from entering his destiny, quenching your Set man through sacrificial service and slaying every other giant that your Set man did not slay.

4. POSITIONING YOURSELF IN THE CORPORATE VISION FIRST AND THEN IN YOUR PERSONAL VISION

The men of David understood that their ability to leave the **cave** (which represented their distress) and enter the **palace** with David (which represented their destiny) was dependent upon their ability to support the vision of their Set man David and to walk with him through the wilderness until the promises of God over his life had been fulfilled (by David sitting on the throne as king).

Whether it is in our families, corporate organizations, churches, communities and nations, there will be a leader whom God will have appointed and God will give that leader a vision. Our ability to connect and submit to that leader's vision and help him fulfil it will be crucial.

2 Samuel 5:1-5 - Then all the tribes of Israel came to David at Hebron and spoke, saying, "Indeed we are your bone and your flesh. ² Also, in time past, when Saul was king over us, you were the one who led Israel out and brought them in; and the Lord said to you, 'You shall shepherd My people Israel, and be ruler over Israel." ³ Therefore all the elders of Israel came to the king at Hebron, and King David made a covenant with them at Hebron before the Lord. And they anointed David king over Israel. ⁴ David was thirty years old when he began to reign, and he reigned forty years. ⁵ In Hebron he reigned over Judah seven years and six months, and in Jerusalem he reigned thirty-three years over all Israel and Judah.

Correct functioning comes under the correct cover and spiritual authority, and an understanding that the corporate vision comes first before your personal vision. Collective responsibility and corporate testing comes first then personal and individual testing follows. Your set man's Destiny comes first then your individual Destiny falls into place. Corporate benefits come as a result of having undergone corporate testing.

David and his men had suffered together, taken responsibilities together, incurred liabilities together and they were now ready to partake of the benefits corporately.

The story of David and his men shows us that before we address our individual visions; we need to address the bigger picture, i.e. the corporate vision and plan as given to the set man or the vision bearer.

The men of David got this revelation very clearly and became totally committed and determined to push David to his destiny (namely to be established as King on the throne at Hebron) according to the word of God through Prophet Samuel.

This is not intended to belittle your own individual and personal vision and destiny, because when you commit to and position yourself to fulfilling the corporate vision given to your set man, you will inevitably and concurrently fulfil your own vision and destiny.

In other words, both the corporate vision and the personal vision are interwoven but there is a divine order whereby the corporate vision needs to be addressed first. More radically put, it will be very difficult or even impossible to fulfil your own personal vision, if you neglect to position yourself strategically under your set man for the fulfilment of the corporate vision. You will end up doing rounds in the wilderness.

If you catch and walk in this revelation, you will be delivered from so much pain, confusion and disappointment regarding your destiny. Equipped with this revelation, the men of David went through a character transformation matured through loyalty and submission, focus and commitment, to their set man and the corporate vision.

You must be careful to remain positioned in the corporate vision diligently and faithfully playing your part otherwise God will assign other people to the set man to come and finish the journey to Destiny. So, watch out because God's plan can never be thwarted or delayed by your refusal to play your part in the corporate vision. You cannot purport to be loyal, submissive and committed to your set man if you are not loyal, submitted and committed to the corporate vision given to your set man by God.

The set man and the corporate vision God has given him are one.

5. POSITIOINING YOURSELF FOR TRANSITION AND FOR YOUR NEXT LEVEL

(1 Samuel 30:1-4) - Now it happened, when David and his men came to Ziklag, on the third day, that the Amalekites had invaded the South and Ziklag, attacked Ziklag and burned it with fire, ² and had taken captive the women and those who were there, from small to great; they did not kill anyone, but carried them away and went their way. ³ So David and his men came to the city, and there it was, burned with fire; and their wives, their sons, and their daughters had been taken captive. ⁴ Then David and the people who were with him lifted up their voices and wept, until they had no more power to weep.

At Ziklag, a crisis arose and David and his men faced their toughest test on the "eve" of their entry to the palace. The devastation and trauma of Ziklag threatened to abort their entry to the palace just when they were at the verge of entering.

Often when we are at the brink of laying hold of our miracle and God's promises, something happens and our ability to respond to that crisis will make us or break us. Their greatest strength (namely their focus and single-mindedness) had become their greatest weakness i.e., their area of greatest anointing was challenged at Ziklag and they panicked and despaired.

They had been strong for so long and had become battle fatigued. When you reach your Ziklag in your moving from distress to destiny remember, it is the last battle before the palace, so hold on.

1 Samuel 30:19 - And nothing of theirs was lacking, either small or great, sons or daughters, spoil or anything which they had taken from them; David recovered all.

However, after overcoming that Ziklag experience, the lessons that were reinforced in David's men where loyalty and submission to the set man, focus and commitment to the corporate vision and that their set man must be positioned in his call and vision in order to strengthen them and offer them leadership during critical moments.

Their initial hasty decision to stone David because of offense and anger would have been an act of self-sabotage because they could not have reached the palace without David, their Set man. This means that any attempt to abandon our set man as we move from distress to destiny will result in self-sabotage and eventually lead to an abortion of our purpose and destiny.

The men also understood that the burning of Ziklag was in order to transition them to their next level. The fact that the scripture emphasizes that Ziklag was **"burnt with fire"** may also signify that there was a purification, cleansing and sanctification in order to burn away any traces of their past, any strange spirits and habits they had acquired in the wilderness.

Any cave mentality that may have hindered them from completely embracing their future, or which may have hindered them from adopting the mentality, protocols and etiquettes of the palace had to be burnt.

Ziklag is never your final destination, and it is a holding position where you are in a waiting mode and paused before entering your next level so you cannot get emotionally bound to Ziklag. Ziklag can become a comfort zone and a place of false security and complacency and it must therefore be burnt to move you from a place of distress to destiny.

You must learn to arise out of Ziklag and offload all past pain, woundedness and every other emotion or mindset that can hinder your transition to the palace. Ziklag is a place of transition to your promotion, your harvest, your reward, your prize, your victory and your breakthrough so you must let go of your Ziklag when time comes.

Transitions can be painful and uncomfortable because they often come to usher us into the unfamiliar with added responsibilities and expectations that may overwhelm us. David would now lead a nation whereas he had led a small band of men in the wilderness, and it is understandable how he might have felt somewhat inadequate.

Perhaps one of the reasons why God enabled David and his men to pursue, overtake and recover all, after the Ziklag ambush, was to revive their self-confidence since he did not want them to enter the palace unsure of themselves, without confidence.

They had not realized that the burning of Ziklag was for purposes of transitioning them to their next level. Whenever we don't have a revelation of what God is doing in our lives, we have a tendency of panicking in fear and doubt just like these men did.

However, inquiring of God constantly and remaining sensitive to the leading of the holy spirit will enable us to know the direction in which God is taking us and even when we do not know what God is doing, will have peace to trust him.

David was a wise man and the process in the wilderness had sharpened him to understand that we must always sow into our next level that God is ushering us into. After Ziklag, David knew he was headed to the throne at Hebron and he knew that he would need valuable allies and support and hence the reason he decided to send some of the spoils after Ziklag to the elders of Judah and elders in other cities.

1st Sam 30: 26-31 – ²⁶ Now when David came to Ziklag, he sent some of the spoil to the elders of Judah, to his friends, saying, "Here is a present for you from the spoil of the enemies of the Lord" ²⁷ to those who were in Bethel, those who were in Ramoth of the South, those who were in Jattir, ²⁸ those who were in Aroer, those who were in Siphmoth, those who were in Eshtemoa, ²⁹ those who were in Rachal, those who were in the cities of the Jerahmeelites, those who were in the cities of the Kenites, ³⁰ those who were in Hormah, those who were in [e]Chorashan, those who were in Athach, ³¹ those who were in Hebron, and to all the places where David himself and his men were accustomed to rove.)

Sowing for where you are going and investing in your next season and level will guarantee you the harvest you want to reap in that next level. David sent some of the recovered loot to the elders of Judah and to the elders in the other cities because he knew that his entry into Hebron would need allies, strategic alliances and relationships.

David understood that those who had helped him reach the palace may not have the capacity to sustain him in the palace, and he would need additional relationships.

You may need some new divine connections and new anointings for your next level (the palace) especially since new levels come with new devils. David knew he would need favour and support from the key people of influence as he entered Hebron so he wisely invested in those relationships. Like David we must be strategic thinkers when moving from distress to destiny.

David's wisdom in sowing into the elders reaped him a mighty harvest when those elders gathered to anoint him King at Hebron.

6. POSITIONING YOURSELF FOR NAMING AS A MIGHTY MAN

1 Chronicles 11:10 - Now these were the heads of the mighty men whom David had, who strengthened themselves with him in his kingdom, with all Israel, to make him king, according to the word of the Lord concerning Israel.

Our naming and defining will often come after we have undergone some spiritual circumcision whereby, we have been moulded through a painful process of removing and uprooting whatever is not useful in us and whatever might hinder us from laying hold of our promises.

2 Samuel 23:8-12 - These are the names of the mighty men whom David had: Josheb-Basshebeth the Tachmonite, chief among the captains. He was called Adino the Eznite, because he had killed eight hundred men at one time. 9 And after him was Eleazar the son of Dodo, the Ahohite, one of the three mighty men with David when they defied the Philistines who were gathered there for battle, and the men of Israel had retreated. 10 He arose and attacked the Philistines until his hand was weary, and his hand stuck to the sword. The Lord brought about a great victory that day; and the people returned after him only to plunder. 11 And after him was Shammah the son of Agee the Hararite. The Philistines had gathered together into a troop where there was a piece of ground full of lentils. So, the people fled from the Philistines. 12 But he stationed himself in the middle of the field, defended it, and killed the Philistines. So, the Lord brought about a great victory.

The naming by David of his mighty men came when he (Set-man) entered Hebron, his "promised land" i.e., the place of fulfilment of God's promises over his life, the awaited throne. The naming and assigning of the roles and positions came after they had undergone a process of purging and circumcision in the wilderness.

Character formation had taken place within them. It was necessary for David (Set-man) to name his men as he strategized his administration and laid down structures that would ensure effective governance and leadership, effective management of the resources that God was releasing to the set man for the fulfilment of God's purposes.

Many set men fail to realise their full potential or they delay fulfilment of their God given vision because of failure to lay and put down and create appropriate structures to handle the blessings God has poured i.e., if God fulfils his promise for lucrative positions and appointments, business deals etc. and you don't have the right structures, you will miss the outpouring of God's blessings.

Naming depends on what you've birthed, while in the wilderness, the men of David had developed certain strengths and the talents and gifting within them as they were nurtured by their Set-man.

A level 5 leader first gets the right people in his bus, sitting on the right seats before deciding the direction to take the bus. This principle of **"first who then where"** is a fundamental for great leadership, according to Jim Collins in his best seller. **"From Good To Great"** Once the right people are sitting on the right seats then your vision, business, ministry, organization etc. can move to its destination and purpose.

So too the men of David had been transformed and could now be named the **"mighty men"** of David in his army and in his administration in the palace, each man according to his gift and strength. A good leader and set man must name and position his men, otherwise his men will strive for positions in the palace and kill each other in confusion. So as soon as David saw he would be established on the throne at Hebron, he begun to line up his men.

- **The Qualities of a Mighty Man**

In order to move from distress to destiny we must be like the men of David and emulate them by understanding what traits and qualities they possessed that enabled them to rebrand from distressed debtors to such mighty men.

i. **They were skilled** in using the sword very able in using the weapons at their disposal and qualified as great warriors in battle. This symbolizes our knowledge of the right correct doctrine, accurate handling of scriptures and interpretation. Rightly dividing the word of God. We must be mighty men and women, immersed in the word of God and mighty in prayer and spiritual warfare.

ii. **They had unparalleled courage** in Battle fearless and bold e.g., the 3 men who broke through the garrison of the Philistine to get to the well of Bethlehem and refresh their set man David with a cup of water, symbolizing that our loyalty to our Set man must be fierce and unwavering and we should be ready to risk our lives in refreshing them. **2 Samuel 23:8-39**

iii. **They fought from the center** of the battle. They stood in the middle of the battle field i.e., not fighting from the side but right in the center of it. Symbolizing our clarity of focus, purpose, vision, intention and commitment. We must confront issues head on not skirt around them in fear and doubt.

iv. **They disarmed the enemy** and stripped the dead and looted from those they killed. Symbolizing that the wealth of the wicked will come to the righteous if we disarm and strip the enemy of everything that God has promised us. **2 Samuel 23:10**

v.   **They secured food provision,** defended the field full of lentils barley demonstrating their ability to feed themselves and others. We must also be people who will be proactive in feeding ourselves and others by guarding the preaching of the gospel of our Lord Jesus Christ which is our bread, our meat and our source of life. **2 Samuel 23:11**

vi. **They showed endurance and perseverance** - went down a pit on snowy day and killed a lion. This shows being all in as regards commitment. Symbolizing that we should be sold out and deeply invested in that which God has called us to do. **2 Samuel 23:20-21**

vii. **They made their enemies their footstool,** one of David's men killed the huge Egyptian with the Egyptian's own sword which he snatched from the Egyptian i.e., the mighty men killed their enemies using the enemies' own weapons showing great strategy and skill. Symbolizing that we should also be able to outsmart our enemies by overturning their wicked strategies and devices against us. **2 Samuel 23:21**

viii. **They applied faith and works;** they could use both their right and left hands during battle. Symbolizing that our one hand represented spiritual power and strength and our other hand represented physical power and strength i.e., faith and works together showing our resourcefulness and balance. **1 Chronicles 12:2**

ix. **They gave support to their Set man for expansion,** they gave David's kingship strong support to extend it over the whole land as the Lord had promised i.e., expanding the set man's influence over every aspect ordained by God. Symbolizing our contribution to our Setman's Destiny, whether through service, resources, prayer etc.

x. **They were armed with Bows and Arrows**, slings and stones showing their readiness for service, in and out of season. Symbolizing that we must be alert always in the spirit armed with the word of God and prayer. **1 Chronicles 12:2**

- **Sonship By Adoption**

The next thing after understanding the qualities these men possessed is to understand the place and role of those who are **adopted by** the set man as opposed to being birthed by the set man. There were those men who were with David from the very beginning so in essence he birthed and moulded them but there were also others who had been birthed by Saul and by other leaders who later joined David and he adopted them.

(1st Chron.12:1-2 "Now these were the men who came to David at Ziklag while he was still a fugitive from Saul the son of Kish; and they were among the mighty men, helpers in the war, 2 armed with bows, using both the right hand and the left in hurling stones and shooting arrows with the bow. They were of Benjamin, Saul's brethren")

Some men joined David while he was still in the wilderness and David received them, some had defected from elsewhere. Your set man will adopt some people who are birthed elsewhere and such adopted sons will have to adapt to the culture of the set man's household

As an adoptee, your reasons and motives must be clear. Is your season over where you were before? Are you carrying baggage like bitterness, offences, woundedness, critical, judgemental spirits or spirits of entitlement? Have you truly discerned and recognized that David is the real move of God or are you just revenging against your former set man?

Some adoptees bring defilement, some come to spy or to suck and drain the set man's anointing and strength selfishly for their own selfish motives. Many adoptees who joined David were already leaders (Pastors with congregations and followings) yet they still submitted under David and to his vision and to that extent they positioned themselves in the corporate vision.

Adoptees should not join Setman expecting front row seats, positions and privileges. They should come ready to serve and their place. David attracted strong people with value and varied gifts, great skills, talents etc. As an adoptee you must recognize the value that the set man will add to your Destiny and life instead of boasting what value you are adding to him.

You are the protégé and he is the leader and vision bearer. Those already around the set man (when receiving the adoptees) must be open and not insecure BUT they have a duty (with pure hearts) to protect the set man from those coming in with wrong motives.

Some adoptees (whose hearts/motives are pure may climb very quickly and may have been brought by God to fill voids that are empty such as roles, duties and responsibilities which those already who there are not performing because of a familiarity or complacency spirit.

7. POSITIONING YOURSELF FOR THE PALACE

a) Keep Your Focus On The Main Goal

The men of David had learnt to narrow their vision to a tunnel vision, they had learnt to keep the main thing the main thing, consistency and discipline, to understand their strengths and weaknesses, total focus and commitment on their main goal (palace at Hebron).

The men of David were of one mind to make David King and they remained focused on that.

1 Chronicles 12:38 - *All these men of war, who could keep ranks, came to Hebron with a loyal heart, to make David king over all Israel; and all the rest of Israel were of one mind to make David king.*

They kept this single mindedness and focus throughout the wilderness as they journeyed and it is only in Ziklag that their trust was momentarily broken until they regained it.

b) Beware of the fear of embracing your promise which is a hindrance to entering your palace.

2 Sam 2:1 - It happened after this that David inquired of the Lord, saying, "Shall I go up to any of the cities of Judah?" And the Lord said to him, "Go up." David said, "Where shall I go up?" And He said, "To Hebron."

David (in the course of time) enquired of God whether he should go to Hebron… which was surprising since the prophetic promise and word had been very clear, and David had waited so long, for the fulfilment of this promise and he had paid such a high price to get here, so why was he hesitant and asking God for confirmation.

This **fear** of embracing your promise is a **trap** by the enemy and a last attempt to stop you laying hold of your promises by second-guessing God's word and promise. It is the "analysis paralysis" where we become awestruck when the promise whether it be a promotion, marriage, the birth of a baby or a financial breakthrough etc. finally manifests and we hesitate in embracing it.

The corporate purpose of Israel gets fulfilled through David entering Hebron and being made King. The distressed men had been transformed through character moulding so now they could be positioned to serve in the highest office in the land.

2 Samuel 2:2-7 ² So David went up there, and his two wives also, Ahinoam the Jezreelitess, and Abigail the widow of Nabal the Carmelite. ³ And David brought up the men who were with him, every man with his household. So, they dwelt in the cities of Hebron.

⁴ Then the men of Judah came, and there they anointed David king over the house of Judah. And they told David, saying, "The men of Jabesh Gilead were the ones who buried Saul."

⁵ So David sent messengers to the men of Jabesh Gilead, and said to them, "You are blessed of the Lord, for you have shown this kindness to your lord, to Saul, and have buried him. ⁶ And now may the Lord show kindness and truth to you. I also will repay you this kindness, because you have done this thing. ⁷ Now therefore, let your hands be strengthened, and be valiant; for your master Saul is dead, and also the house of Judah has anointed me king over them."

There is power in right positioning, so as you move from distress to destiny your positioning will be crucial.

CHAPTER 5

The Power of Focus

From Slavery and Oppression To Inheritance and Ownership - Story Of Joshua and Caleb

Chapter Preview

1. A "Grasshopper Mentality" Will Keep You In The Wilderness

2. "The Fear of Giants" Will Rob Your Inheritance

3. "Emotional Ties" Will Blur Your Focus and Vision

4. "Spiritual Rebellion" Will Lead to Spiritual Leprosy

5. "Emotional Burnout" Can Cost You a Destiny

OPENING REMARKS

Moving from distress to Destiny entails embarking on the road to your establishment. It means leaving a place of **bondage, slavery** and **oppression** to your promised land.

(Exodus 6:10-11) *And the Lord spoke to Moses, saying, [11] "Go in, tell Pharaoh King of Egypt to let the children of Israel go out of his land."*

To be established means to ratify, confirm, ordain; settle, approve, fix, be founded, **"Guwn"** in Hebrew to rise up, to grow up, mature up to strengthen, to succeed you.

Your promised land is your place of establishment, ownership, new dimension of life, abundance, influence and impact, where you fulfil God's plan and purpose for your life and lay hold of the promises and inheritance God has for you.

Each one of us has their own promised land; i.e., that place and sphere, where you have been called to reign, rule and have a voice and influence over, so that you exert godly influence there e.g., politics and governance, business and economy, media, education, arts and entertainment, family and church.

Once you are established, you govern which means to rule, reign, take charge and control of your affairs, exercise authority and influence and be a voice over your sphere and ordained place. In other words, being established means you become the who you were born to be, and you do what you were created to do where you were created to do it.

When the children of Israel left Egypt towards Canaan, they encountered a myriad of obstacles, and it took great determination for those who finally crossed over even as many died in the wilderness. Those who endured were established in the inheritance that God had promised them.

In 2nd Sam.5:12 *"So David knew that the Lord had established him as king over Israel, and that He had exalted His kingdom for the sake of His people Israel."*

David knew and perceived that God had **"established"** him King over Israel. Jacob also got **established** in his place of promise when he obeyed God and returned to Bethel from uncle Laban's and Ruth and Naomi also got **established** when they also obeyed God and returned to Bethlehem from Moab.

In 1ˢᵗ **Peter.5:10** *"But may the God of all grace, who called us to His eternal glory by Christ Jesus, after you have suffered a while, perfect, establish, strengthen, and settle you."*

You become **established** in righteousness, from oppression, from fear and conflict etc. Notice that establishing comes after you have suffered awhile meaning after you have been in distress, God begins to move you, to strengthen you, perfect you and settle you in your place of destiny.

In the Book Isaiah God promises to move us from tempest terror, fear and oppression which all signify distress and to establish us in peace, security and righteousness which all signify a place of destiny.

(Isaiah 54:11-14) - *"O you afflicted one, tossed with tempest, and not comforted, Behold, I will lay your stones with colourful gems, And lay your foundations with sapphires. I will make your pinnacles of rubies, Your gates of crystal, And all your walls of precious stones. All your children shall be taught by the Lord, And great shall be the peace of your children. ¹⁴ In righteousness you shall be established; You shall be far from oppression, for you shall not fear; And from terror, for it shall not come near you."*

When God is establishing us by moving us from distress to destiny, he also establishes our hearts in love and in holiness as we see in,

1st Thess.3:12-13 *"And may the Lord make you increase and abound in love to one another and to all, just as we do to you, so that He may establish your hearts blameless in holiness before our God and Father at the coming of our Lord Jesus Christ with all His saints."*

Moving from distress to destiny is a journey and a process with many road blocks and hindrances but God will always make a way if we trust and obey him and we will certainly be established in our Promised Land and place of destiny.

The story of Moses and the children of Israel as God delivered them from Egypt (their place of distress) and begun to usher them into the wilderness towards their promised land (their place of destiny) is a classic example and demonstration of the obstacles and hindrances we often face. In particular Moses and the Israelites encountered 5 major road blocks and hindrances which they needed to overcome:

1. The grasshopper mentality
2. The fear of giants
3. Spiritual Leprosy
4. Emotional Ties
5. Emotional Burnout

If we are serious about moving from our places of distress to our destiny, we must overcome these obstacles, by maintaining our focus on the promises of land, walking by faith and trusting God.

1. "THE GRASSHOPPER MENTALITY" WILL KEEP YOU IN THE WILDERNESS

The grasshopper mentality is an internal hindrance within us that will often delay and derail us in our journey to destiny. The children of Israel described themselves as grasshoppers in.

(Numbers 13:33) *There we saw the giants (the descendants of Anak came from the giants); and we were like grasshoppers in our own sight, and so we were in their sight."*

The characteristics, traits and nature of a grasshopper are interesting, a grass hopper eats soft leaves symbolizing weakness and an inability to handle tough issues. It blends in the background and becomes camouflaged symbolizing a crowd mentality and an inability to form your own opinions.

This fear of standing up for your beliefs and values arises from a fear of criticism and fear of people's opinion. A grasshopper hops all over the place meaning that if you have a grasshopper mentality you will be a **"church hopper"** unable to settle, serve and be loyal to any one church or fellowship or spiritual authority and godly leadership.

One of the most interesting things about grasshoppers is that **"grasshoppers do not eat grapes."** So, although they will land on the grapes, they don't eat them and instead they just eat the leaves. This symbolizes the inability to recognize and feed on that which is valuable or inability to see your opportunities and resources when you are right on top of them.

This grasshopper mentality is what plagued the children of Israel as they journeyed from Egypt to Canaan through the wilderness when God decided to move them from their place of distress to their promised land and destiny.

The children of Israel came to the border and edge of the promised land i.e., they came to the eve of their breakthrough but missed it and only a few of them made it into their promised inheritance. The spies actually stepped on the promised land but came back to die in the wilderness. This is the tragedy of those with a grasshopper mentality. The spies agreed with God that the promised land existed and it was very good, but they did not believe that they were good enough to possess it.

The Symptoms of a Grasshopper Mentality

This grasshopper mentality leads to an identity crisis characterised by

- **low self-esteem**, not knowing who you are
- **low self-confidence** whereby you doubt the call of God upon your life,
- **low self-worth** whereby you doubt the gifting and anointing within you,
- **low self-respect** whereby you believe others are better than you and so you allow others to misuse you for their own selfish agendas,
- **"Spiritual amnesia"** whereby you forget the mighty works and power of your God and the miracles he has already done in your life.

The children of Israel forgot the Red Sea miracle.

What Causes This Grasshopper Mentality?

i.   When you lack sufficient faith and trust in God's promises.

ii. Overstaying in the wilderness until you forgot where you were going.

iii. When your character has not yet been moulded, so you don't have a firm foundation, to withstand the trials and hardships.

iv. When the word, promise and prophecy takes so long to manifest you begin to get used to the manna, and you settle for less or just enough.

v.   Not doing what God called you to do-until you forget what it was. In other words, when you procrastinate in embarking and fulfilling your purpose, you will eventually lose your momentum.

vi. When God seems to be taking too long in ushering you into your Call and Purpose. You go into panic mode like Sarah and you decide to help God and produce an Ishmael instead of patiently waiting for your Isaac.

vii. It is often as a result of no affirmation and no endorsement by those you expect to affirm and endorse you like parents, leaders etc.

2. "FEAR OF GIANTS" WILL ROB YOUR INHERITANCE

Numbers 13:31-33 - But the men who had gone up with him said, "We are not able to go up against the people, for they are stronger than we." [32] And they gave the children of Israel a bad report of the land which they had spied out, saying, "The land through which we have gone as spies is a land that devours its inhabitants, and all the people whom we saw in it are men of great stature. [33] There we saw the giants (the descendants of Anak came from the giants); and we were like grasshoppers in our own sight, and so we were in their sight."

When you have been too long in the wilderness, you lose confidence and you begin to think that you don't have what it takes because the sacrifice looks too high and the "giants" look too intimidating.

- Don't ignore your giants whether external or internal. You should acknowledge the giants without denial because only then will you be able to deal with them. Always confront the brutal facts of your current reality but without losing faith that you can overcome any adversity.

- Recognize and confront the Giants because you have what it takes to slay them. God had already assured the children of Israel that He would enable them to defeat and displace the giants so all they needed to do was to trust God.

- Watch your words and how you define yourself. The 10 spies said "We were like grasshoppers in their sight." Your opinion of yourself should be based on what God says about you.

- Daily cultivate the mind of Christ in you to develop a strong positive mindset and a positive self-image. Be like Joshua and Caleb who were not afraid of the Giants

  Numbers 13:30 - Then Caleb quieted the people before Moses, and said, "Let us go up at once and take possession, for we are well able to overcome it."

- Get rid of the grasshopper complex and acquire a Giant slayer complex. The Israelites had been victims in the wilderness for so long until they had developed a **"wilderness paralysis"** whereby they got stuck in the wilderness.

Often past pain and childhood traumas can also cause this grasshopper mentality and identity crisis. The children of Israel had been through a lot and they were still suffering from the memory and trauma of bondage and oppression in Egypt, so they feared that the giants would also oppress them and enslave them.

Sometimes if you have been abused or oppressed in the past, you will often walk in fear of repeated abuse and oppression, for example, where you experienced abuse and oppression in a previous relationship or marriage or even in your workplace, you will often be hesitant and fearful of any situation or relationship that you think may repeat that abuse and oppression.

Doubt and unbelief also tormented the children of Israel, so that no matter how clear God's promises were, they lacked the capacity to fully embrace and lay hold of them, and so when God instructed them through Moses to enter and possess the promised land, they insisted on first scouting it instead of taking God at His word.

It is possible that God's plan and intention was for the Israelites to just arise and possess the land and maybe scouting the land was not actually God's original idea, but it was the people who acted fearful and insisted on wanting to scout the land first, so God agreed to indulge their doubt and unbelief.

(Numbers 13:1-4) And the Lord spoke to Moses, saying, ² "Send men to spy out the land of Canaan, which I am giving to the children of Israel; from each tribe of their fathers, you shall send a man, everyone a leader among them." ³ So Moses sent them from the Wilderness of Paran according to the command of the Lord, all of them men who were heads of the children of Israel. ⁴ Now these were their names: from the tribe of Reuben, Shammua the son of Zaccur.

It is interesting to note that this idea of scouting the land was also as a result of their eroded confidence in Moses leadership after Miriam questioned Moses's decision concerning his Cushite wife. This sin by Miriam eroded the integrity and credibility of Moses's leadership in the eyes of the people (so even though God punished her with leprosy) it was soon after Miriam had challenged Moses that the people insisted on scouting the land instead of arising and possessing it as per God's instruction through Moses.

(Numbers 12:1) Then Miriam and Aaron spoke against Moses because of the Ethiopian woman whom he had married; for he had married an Ethiopian woman.

3. "EMOTIONAL TIES" WILL BLUR YOUR FOCUS AND VISION

Moses was to blame for not dealing with Miriam's insubordination because he was emotionally bound, he allowed emotional ties to derail him from his spiritual assignment that God had given him which involved the Destinies of so many people.

Never let family or emotional ties and friendships derail you from your establishment. Even Jesus said his mother and brothers should not derail him from the assignment God had given him.

Moses had a soft-spot for his sister Miriam and hence the reason he was emotionally blinded to her sinful behaviour of disrespect and insubordination.

The people around you in your inner circle must be able to set an example and follow your leadership, not incite the people and erode your credibility, integrity and your influence over people. This is because the people you are leading can never benefit from the grace and anointing upon your life if they doubt and dishonour your leadership and authority.

Moses failed to discern the first seed of rebellion in Miriam at the Red Sea when Miriam led the people in her own song of victory after Moses had already led the people in worship following the Red Sea victory.

Exodus 15:20 - Then Miriam the prophetess, the sister of Aaron, took the timbrel in her hand; and all the women went out after her with timbrels and with dances.

This was not the first time Miriam would derail Moses's mission and God's plan. This time the people delayed entering the promised land because of Miriam's leprosy (Sin) since they had to wait for her to heal

Numbers 12:15 - So Miriam was shut out of the camp seven days, and the people did not journey till Miriam was brought in **again**

Then the other time

Numbers 20:1 - Then the children of Israel, the whole congregation, came into the Wilderness of Zin in the first month, and the people stayed in Kadesh; and Miriam died there and was buried there.

When Miriam died and her death must have affected Moses and obviously delayed the journey to the promised land as they buried her before moving on.

Sometimes rebellion had to be very subtle and almost unnoticeable. At this point Moses was clearly the designated senior pastor and prophet and after he had finished the service at the Red Sea, Miriam had no business picking her tambourine and reopening the service.

Numbers 12:13 - So Moses cried out to the Lord, saying, "Please heal her, O God, I pray!"

Moses pleaded with God to heal Miriam of leprosy; despite the negative influence she was having on the people.

Never stand in God's way when he is dealing with sin in the camp. Therefore, Moses's failure to deal with and discipline

Miriam's behaviour threatened and delayed their journey to their establishment and Destiny. Miriam was punished by God publicly as a lesson to the others.

Sadly, Miriam's greatest strength became her greatest weakness because while previously she had been Moses greatest supporter but now became his greatest critic. Your Moses may not hear you criticizing him but God does hear you.

Miriam began so well but finished so badly, because she allowed her emotions to get in the way.

Miriam had become over familiar with Moses, possibly because she had protected him while he was a little boy, but she failed to see that this was not the same Moses. He had undergone a metamorphosis and the fire of God, when he had ascended the mountain of God and he had been empowered with the rod of God meaning God's authority.

Moses had become her leader and spiritual authority and not her little brother, but Miriam had forgotten this and that her destiny was hidden in that little boy she had once protected.

Often when you help someone get to the top, you are helping yourself because that person's success is intended to activate something in you about your destiny hence the reason you have been positioned there, as a ladder holder to help that person fulfil God's mission.

We must also remember to respect and honour the "office" of leadership, irrespective of the person holding that office and we must not allow our emotional ties and relationships to that leader to distort our image of them.

4. "SPIRITUAL REBELLION" WILL LEAD TO SPIRITUAL LEPROSY

Numbers 12:1-15, *Then Miriam and Aaron spoke against Moses because of the Ethiopian woman whom he had married; for he had married an Ethiopian woman.* [2] *So they said, "Has the Lord indeed spoken only through Moses? Has He not spoken through us also?" And the Lord heard it.* [3] *(Now the man Moses was very humble, more than all men who were on the face of the earth.)* [4] *Suddenly the Lord said to Moses, Aaron, and Miriam, "Come out, you three, to the tabernacle of meeting!" So, the three came out.* [5] *Then the*

Lord came down in the pillar of cloud and stood in the door of the tabernacle, and called Aaron and Miriam. And they both went forward. ⁶Then He said, "Hear now My words: If there is a prophet among you, I, the Lord, make Myself known to him in a vision; I speak to him in a dream.⁷Not so with My servant Moses; He is faithful in all My house.⁸I speak with him face to face, even plainly, and not in dark sayings; And he sees the form of the Lord. Why then were you not afraid to speak against My servant Moses?" ⁹So the anger of the Lord was aroused against them, and He departed. ¹⁰And when the cloud departed from above the tabernacle, suddenly Miriam became leprous, as white as snow. Then Aaron turned toward Miriam, and there she was, a leper. ¹¹So Aaron said to Moses, "Oh, my lord! Please do not lay this sin on us, in which we have done foolishly and in which we have sinned. ¹²Please do not let her be as one dead, whose flesh is half consumed when he comes out of his mother's womb!" ¹³So Moses cried out to the Lord, saying, "Please heal her, O God, I pray!" ¹⁴Then the Lord said to Moses, "If her father had but spit in her face, would she not be shamed seven days? Let her be shut out of the camp seven days, and afterward she may be received again." ¹⁵So Miriam was shut out of the camp seven days, and the people did not journey till Miriam was brought in again

- Leprosy is a very infectious disease which attacks the skin symbolizing your spiritual garments which is basically your salvation, your testimony and your walk with God and your ability to walk in holiness and righteousness.

- It attacks your **eyes** symbolizing your vision and your ability to receive spiritual revelation.

- It attacks your **ears** symbolizing your ability to hear God.

- It attacks you **nose** symbolizing your inability to discern things in the spirit.

- Leprosy makes you lose feeling in your **hands** and **fingers** symbolizing an attack on your strength, an inability to work, create wealth or exercise power effectively, and also symbolises an inability to do battle in prayer and wage war.

(Psalms 144:1) *Blessed be the Lord my Rock, Who trains my hands for war, And my fingers for battle*

Physical leprosy is a very infectious disease and if not handled properly, it can infect the entire camp, so anyone who got leprosy was ostracized and kept outside the camp away from the people until they had healed. Spiritual leprosy symbolizes an isolation, discrimination and disconnecting from valuable destiny relationships in your life thereby delaying your move from distress to destiny until you have sufficiently healed.

In the Old Testament leprosy was a sign of judgement following sin and, in this situation, Miriam was being punished for rebelling against the servant of God. Gehazi was inflicted with leprosy for the sin of greed for material things when he disobeyed his master Elisha and took the gifts from the Shunammite woman that Elisha had instructed him not to take.

2 Kings 5:27 - Therefore the leprosy of Naaman shall cling to you and your descendants forever." And he went out from his presence **leprous,** *as* **white** *as snow.*

King Uzziah was also inflicted with leprosy for the sin of disobedience and pride as a punishment for burning incense which was only supposed to be burnt by consecrated priests.

2 Kings 15:5 - Then the Lord struck the king, so that he was a leper until the day of his death; so, he dwelt in an isolated house. And Jotham the king's son was over the royal house, judging the people of the land.

We must therefore guard against spiritual leprosy by ensuring that we do not develop greed for possessions, a rebellious spirit against authority or pride and disobedience.

5. "EMOTIONAL BURNOUT" CAN COST YOU A DESTINY

Another obstacle we may encounter when moving from distress to destiny is burnout and meltdown.

(Numbers 20:11) *Then Moses lifted his hand and struck the rock twice with his rod; and water came out abundantly, and the congregation and their animals drank.*

At the border and edge of the promised land Moses completely fell apart and snapped, he struck the rock instead of speaking to it, in other words Moses misused his rod which symbolised the authority God had placed upon him. Often in our journey to being established in Destiny from distress we become overwhelmed, battle fatigued and weary. This may lead to an emotional burnout and mental meltdown. To truly understand and appreciate Moses's emotional meltdown and burnout; you need to remember his background.

- He escaped death as a baby when there were death threats by Pharoah and his mother had to put him in a basket in the river to protect him, hoping for someone to find the baby and raise him.

- Her prayer was answered when Pharaoh's daughter found baby Moses and drew him out of the river and raised him as her own.

- He was raised in Pharaoh's palace as an Egyptian prince under the Egyptian culture even though he was a Hebrew.

- He killed an Egyptian when protecting a Jew, so he had to flee from Pharaoh's palace into the wilderness.

Exodus 2:11-12 - Now it came to pass in those days, when Moses was grown, that he went out to his brethren and looked at their burdens. And he saw an Egyptian beating a Hebrew, one of his brethren. ¹² So he looked this way and that way, and when he saw no one, he killed the Egyptian and hid him in the sand.

- God moulded him in the wilderness of Jethro for many years until God felt he was ready and he commissioned him to deliver the children of Israel from their slavery and bondage in Egypt, at the burning bush experience.

Exodus 3:2-6 - And the Angel of the Lord appeared to him in a flame of fire from the midst of a bush. So, he looked, and behold, the bush was burning with fire, but the bush was not consumed. ³ Then Moses said, "I will now turn aside and see this great sight, why the bush does not burn." ⁴ So when the Lord saw that he turned aside to look, God called to him from the midst of the bush and said, "Moses, Moses!" And he said, "Here I am." ⁵ Then He said, "Do not draw near this place. Take your sandals off your feet, for the place where you stand is holy ground." ⁶ Moreover He said, "I am the God of your father—the God of Abraham, the God of Isaac, and the God of Jacob." And Moses hid his face, for he was afraid to look upon God

- Once he accepted his call, he became so passionate and committed and he engaged Pharoah tenaciously until Pharoah finally released the children of Israel.

- Moses had a great victory over Pharaoh at the Red Sea parting when Pharoah changed his mind and pursued Moses and the Israelites.

(Exodus 14:21) *Then Moses stretched out his hand over the sea; and the Lord caused the sea to go back by a strong east wind all that night, and made the sea into dry land, and the waters were divided.*

- Moses had to receive the 10 commandments twice because the first time he came down the mountain with the first tablet, he found the people worshipping a golden calf and he broke the tablet in frustration.

  Exodus 32:19 - So it was, as soon as he came near the camp, that he saw the calf and the dancing. So Moses' anger became hot, and he cast the tablets out of his hands and broke them at the foot of the mountain.

In short therefore Moses had gone through and withstood a lot and it did not help that he had to constantly intercede for the people who were stubborn and stiff-necked pleading with God not to kill them for their rebellion and defiance.

Moses was leading a stubborn, rebellious, stiff-necked people who had rejected the promises of God by their doubt and unbelief (causing them to remain in the wilderness for 40 years more than God had intended) really took its toll on Moses, and eventually led him to have a major emotional meltdown when he got exhausted and burnt out.

Exodus 32:9 - And the Lord said to Moses, "I have seen this people, and indeed it is a stiff-necked people!

Moses remained calm through so many traumatic moments that he must have had so much pent-up tension until he exploded, his love for the people which was initially his greatest strength became his greatest weakness that led to his meltdown. The constant murmurings by the people whenever they encountered a hardship, their stubbornness doubt and unbelief vexed Moses's spirit to breaking point.

When they came to the edge of wilderness again in Numbers 20 and the people murmured because there was no water, we see how calm Moses was as he sought God's directions but then almost without warning he snaps and disobeys God's strict instructions to speak to the rock and instead he struck the rock in anger, an action that cost him dearly.

Numbers 20:7-12 - Then the Lord spoke to Moses, saying, [8] "Take the rod; you and your brother Aaron gather the congregation together. Speak to the rock before their eyes, and it will yield its water; thus, you shall bring water for them out of the rock, and give drink to the congregation and their animals." [9] So Moses took the rod from before the Lord as He commanded him. [10] And Moses and Aaron gathered the assembly together before the rock; and he said to them, "Hear now, you rebels! Must we bring water for you out of this rock?" [11] Then Moses lifted his hand and struck the rock twice with his rod; and water came out abundantly, and the congregation and their animals drank. [12] Then the Lord spoke to Moses and Aaron, "Because you did not believe Me, to hallow Me in the eyes of the children of Israel, therefore you shall not bring this assembly into the land which I have given them."

Emotional burnout is one of the most common reasons that keeps us in distress hindering us from moving to our destiny.

- **Firstly,** it is built up stress, extreme tiredness and fatigue when there are too many demands on you and very high expectations until the **"straw that broke the camel's back"** brings you tumbling down into an emotional mess because after all the stress and tension something relatively small and insignificant pushes you off the edge.

Burnout leads to the loss of incentive and motivation especially where your devotion or something you are very passionate about fails to work out which leads to disappointment and hopelessness

The word "Burnout" was first coined in 1974 by Herbert Freudenberge in his book **"burnout" the cost of high achievement"**

Burnout is long term exhaustion which also arises from taking on and carrying heavy mental and emotional burdens, engaging in relationships that make unrealistic demands on you until you get overworked and worn out, undervalued with no rewards and lack of appreciation and recognition.

Emotional and mental burnout is often associated with high achievers who have a type A personality.

When you suffer from burnout you experience loss of self-value and identity whereby you withdraw from responsibilities and you begin to isolate yourself from your loved ones and people generally.

You start missing church and fellowship, thereby opening yourself up to wrong relationships and attacks by the enemy. This is what happened to Elijah when he found himself under the Juniper tree suffering from a self-pity syndrome completely unable to appreciate and enjoy the victory, he had just had at Mount Carmel.

1 Kings 19:4-5 - But he himself went a day's journey into the wilderness, and came and sat down under a broom tree. And he prayed that he might die, and said, "It is enough! Now, Lord, take my life, for I *am* no better than my fathers!"

⁵ Then as he lay and slept under a broom tree, suddenly an angel touched him, and said to him, "Arise *and* eat."

Sometimes even when we achieve some great victory in our lives, we fail to appreciate it because of what it took to get there and we succumb to having carried too much on our shoulders to get there and we end up burnt-out physically, emotionally and mentally.

- **Secondly**, an emotional burnout can be due to the bad choices and decisions that we may make along the way which lead to taking wrong actions or having a distorted perception.

  This ultimately leads to low emotional intelligence where you are unable to manage your emotions and you have a lack sufficient self-awareness (namely a failure to respond properly to the emotions) of others and to your own emotions which may eventually lead to self-sabotage and you tragically abort your move from distress to destiny.

- **Thirdly**, emotional burnout can occur when your own followers and helpers are not aligned to your vision and they are unable or unwilling to help you to fulfil that vision.

  Moses was so desperate to succeed in his mission and assignment that even when it was out of his control, he forgot that the people's failure was not his failure. Moses was surrounded by "**grasshopper mentality people**".

  The 10 spies were his co-ministers and part of his ministerial team yet they had no capacity to impact the people with hope and instead they were the ones who incited and poisoned the people with doubt and unbelief against God's promises to possess their promised land.

  Numbers 13:31-33 - But the men who had gone up with him said, "We are not able to go up against the people, for they are stronger than we." ³² And they gave the children of Israel a bad report of the land which they had spied out, saying, "The land through which we have gone as spies is a land that devours its inhabitants, and all the people whom we saw in it are men of great stature. ³³ There we saw the giants (the descendants of Anak came from the giants); and we were like grasshoppers in our own sight, and so we were in their sight."

In addition, the lack of a proper eldership structure also contributed to Moses' emotional meltdown because there was no effective delegation. Moses was operating with a one man show mentality and with a lone ranger syndrome. His father-in-law Jethro had to tell Moses to delegate otherwise he was wearing himself out. A proper eldership structure means delegated authority backed up by a leading authority (namely Moses)

(Exodus 18:21-23) Moreover you shall select from all the people able men, such as fear God, men of truth, hating covetousness; and place such over them to be rulers of thousands, rulers of hundreds, rulers of fifties, and rulers of tens. ²² And let them judge the people at all times. Then it will be that every great matter they shall bring to you, but every small matter they themselves shall judge. So, it will be easier for you, for they will bear the burden with you. ²³ If you do this thing, and God so commands you, then you will be able to endure, and all this people will also go to their place in peace."

In summary therefore in order for us to move from distress to destiny, we must overcome any grasshopper mentality that keeps us in the wilderness, our fear of giants that rob us of our inheritance, doubt and unbelief that causes us to miss God's promises, emotional ties that blind us, rebellion that leads to spiritual leprosy, and emotional burnout that leads to an abortion of purpose.

CHAPTER 6

The Power In A Room

From Dead Dreams To Resurrected Miracles –
the story of the Shunammite Woman

Chapter Preview

1. *She Had Discernment*

2. *She Opened Her Heart*

3. *Her Motives Were Pure*

4. *She Had Wisdom*

5. *She Understood Where the Real Anointing Was*

6. *She Had Faith and Trust in God's Power*

7. *She Was Obedient*

OPENING REMARKS

Moving from your distress to your destiny may entail you receiving certain miracles, whether they be as a result of specific promises that God had given you, or as a result of your own desire that aligns with the will of God for you.

It could be as a result of doing something that provokes God to impose certain miracles upon you that you were not expecting nor had you prayed or asked for them.

It could even as a result of something you had desired and prayed for over a long time without it manifesting, until you came to a place where you gave up on it and you learnt to live without it.

Yet somehow God surprises you at a time you least expect by remembering that promise and fulfilling it.

2nd Kings 4:9-10; 15-17 (NKJV) *9 And she said to her husband, "Look now, I know that this is a holy man of God, who passes by us regularly. 10 Please, let us make a small upper room on the wall; and let us put a bed for him there, and a table and a chair and a lampstand; so, it will be, whenever he comes to us, he can turn in there."*

15 So he said, "Call her." When he had called her, she stood in the doorway. 16 Then he said, "About this time next year you shall embrace a son." And she said, "No, my lord. Man of God, do not lie to your maidservant!" 17 But the woman conceived, and bore a son when the appointed time had come, of which Elisha had told her."

The story of the **Shunammite woman** is a classic example of the power in creating room for God in your life and how by doing so you will move from your place of distress into the promises of God and into your destiny.

The **Shunammite woman** by inviting in Elisha and making room for him, she made room for God because Elisha was a servant of God and represented the move of God in that day. She was a noble woman, meaning that she was an honoured and recognized woman who appears to have been well-off in terms of material substance and a comfortable life.

Yet she took time to be involved in the things of God and to be sensitive to the needs of God's servants. Often, once we are in a contented place of comfort it is very easy to become self-absorbed and self-focused and to become insensitive to the things of God.

The **Shunammite woman** did **3 key things** that ushered her into her miracle zone;

a) A Room For Miracles

She made room for her **miracle** and gave birth to a miracle son. Initially the Shunammite woman simply invited Elisha the servant of God for meals but she went a step further by building a permanent room for him.

b) A Resurrection Platform

She laid a platform for the **resurrection** power of God, when her son was resurrected by Elisha in the same room that she had made for Elisha.

2nd **Kings 4:32-33; 36-37 (NKJV)** *"32 When Elisha came into the house, there was the child, lying dead on his bed. 33 He went in therefore, shut the door behind the two of them, and prayed to the LORD." 36 And he called Gehazi and said, "Call this Shunammite woman." So he called her. And when she came in to him, he said, "Pick up your son." 37 So she went in, fell at his feet, and bowed to the ground; then she picked up her son and went out."*

c) A Climate For Restoration

She created a spiritual climate and an atmosphere for her **restoration** after the famine.

2ⁿᵈ Kings 8:5-8 *"⁵ Now it happened, as he was telling the king how he had restored the dead to life, that there was the woman whose son he had restored to life, appealing to the king for her house and for her land. And Gehazi said, "My lord, O king, this is the woman, and this is her son whom Elisha restored to life." ⁶ And when the king asked the woman, she told him. So, the king appointed a certain officer for her, saying, "Restore all that was hers, and all the proceeds of the field from the day that she left the land until now."*

The Shunammite woman possessed **7 qualities** that enabled her to do the above **3 things** that ushered her into her place of destiny.

1. SHE HAD DISCERNMENT

She was sharp, alert spiritually, always on the lookout for an opportunity to sow into the things of God. Notice how her husband did not discern that Elisha was a man of God, meaning that even those close to us may not always discern what we discern in the spirit.

The Shunammite woman simply declared to her husband that Elisha was a man of God so they needed to minister to him by creating a room for him. This means that there are things in the spirit you will have to know that you know without over consulting those around you who may not have the revelation you have.

2. SHE OPENED HER HEART

Despite the fact that she was barren the Shunammite had not developed a spirit of bitterness like many often do in such circumstances and instead she remained a generous sacrificial giver by building an upper room for Elisha.

Sometimes when we are disappointed and feel that God has not come through for us with regard to a certain issue in our lives, we may become hardened and even cynical about the things of God, or about sowing into the things of God perhaps because we feel that we did all that we knew to do for so long and yet we feel that God did not come through for us.

So even though we may not murmur or complain audibly, we slowly and sometimes subconsciously develop that hardness and cynicism. This is what happed to Sarah after she had waited so long for God to fulfil His promise and break her barrenness until she became cynical and even laughed when the angel of God reminded her of the promise.

Genesis 18:12-14 - Therefore Sarah laughed within herself, saying, "After I have grown old, shall I have pleasure, my lord being old also?"

[13] And the Lord said to Abraham, "Why did Sarah laugh, saying, 'Shall I surely bear *a child,* since I am old?' [14] Is anything too hard for the Lord? At the appointed time I will return to you, according to the time of life, and Sarah shall have a son."

By building and creating that upper room for Elisha, the **Shunammite woman** was in essence raising an altar for God, meaning a meeting point where God would have to show up. Every time someone raised an altar in the Old Testament God always showed up e.g., Abraham in Mt. Moriah, Jacob at Bethel, Isaac at Beersheba.

The Shunammite after discerning that Elisha was a man of God in need of a place, where he could rest during his mission proceeded to take **action.**

2 Kings 4: 10 Please, let us make a small upper room on the wall; and let us put a bed for him there, and a table and a chair and a lampstand; so, it will be, whenever he comes to us, he can turn in there."

It was an "**upper**" room, signifying a place of empowerment, a place of prayer, a place for the habitation of God and most importantly it turned out to be a place where God addressed her issue when the prophet Elisha wondered what is it that could be done for the Shunammite woman.

2 Kings 4:15-16 - So he said, "Call her." When he had called her, she stood in the doorway. ¹⁶ Then he said, "About this time next year you shall embrace a son." And she said, "No, my lord. Man of God, do not lie to your maidservant!"

In other words when we create permanent room for God in our lives, we are in essence creating an opportunity for God to address the long-forgotten issues in our lives so that God can address and fulfil them.

Her giving was an act of worship to God and the fact that she **furnished** the room, she was going an extra mile, to sacrificially provide for the man of God (Elisha).

Sometimes when we minister to the servants of God we may be tempted to do "**just enough**" and that which is within our means and comfort, but the Shunammite woman teaches us that there are rewards in going that extra mile, and ministering to God and His servants beyond our comfort zone and with that which will cost us and sacrificially.

Like David said in **1 Chronicles 21:24** that he would not offer to God that which had not cost him.

1 Chronicles 21:24 – Then King David said to Ornan, "No, but I will surely buy *it* for the full price, for I will not take what is yours for the Lord, nor offer burnt offerings with *that which* costs *me* nothing."

The items that the Shunammite woman put in that upper room for Elisha were significant and they played a vital role in the resurrection of her miracle (when her son died).

- **The Table;** symbolized a place of provision, communion, and covenant making, and a place of meeting with God so that He can fulfil His promises to us.

- **The Bed;** symbolized a place of rest meaning that she did not have to panic or become anxious but to remain calm knowing that God would be faithful, a place for the conception and resurrection of her miracle.

- **The Chair;** symbolized a place of authority, meaning the presence of God and the power of God and a place where God would subdue and silence death.

- **The Lamp stand;** which contained oil to enable it to burn and release light symbolizing a place for the anointing and the Spirit of God, and the light symbolized the truth of God meaning that God is not a man that He should lie and having given the Shunammite woman her miracle, God would not allow the enemy to take away that miracle from her.

3. HER MOTIVES WERE PURE

She had no selfish agenda and she just wanted the presence of God, to minister to God and his servant Elisha. She did not rush to request Elisha for any material substance, possession or position. In other words, the miracle chased her because she had made room for it.

2 Kings 4:13-14 – And he said to him, "Say now to her, 'Look, you have been concerned for us with all this care. What *can I* do for you? Do you want me to speak on your behalf to the king or to the commander of the army?'"

She answered, "I dwell among my own people." [14] So he said, "What then *is* to be done for her?" And Gehazi answered, "Actually, she has no son, and her husband is old."

It is unfortunate that often we may attempt to manipulate God and the servants of God in our giving and rendering service with ulterior motives based on our selfish agendas so that our giving and service may not come from a pure heart.

In addition, sometimes we may attempt to control God and His servants in our giving and rendering of service where we do so with strings attached so as to force the hand of God and the hand of his servant to do our bidding that is often not in the will of God.

The **Shunammite woman** was not seeking to control or manipulate the servant of God and this is evidenced by the fact that even when Elisha asked her what could be done for her, she hesitated because favors from the servant of God was not at the front of her mind at all.

4. SHE HAD WISDOM

When her miracle son died; she knew exactly what to do. This shows that by virtue of having positioned herself in the move of God (Elisha) she was able to operate at a high level of wisdom.

2 Kings 4:22-24 - Then she called to her husband, and said, "Please send me one of the young men and one of the donkeys, that I may run to the man of God and come back." [23] So he said, "Why are you going to him today? It is neither the New Moon nor the Sabbath." And she said, "It is well." [24] Then she saddled a donkey, and said to her servant, "Drive, and go forward; do not slacken the pace for me unless I tell you."

It is interesting that the **Shunammite woman** did not panic but she remained calm demonstrating that deep down she knew that God would come through for her. We often get into a panic when something goes wrong and in our panic, we are unable to make the right choices and decisions and we end up making the situation worse.

She laid her dead son on Elisha's bed (not her husband's or her own) because she discerned that the resurrection power of God was on that particular bed and that the room, she had created for Elisha was the contact point for her miracle and the resurrection of her miracle son.

This is a valuable lesson to us, that whenever the miracles God has given, us get attacked by the enemy, we should return to the place (symbolically) where God gave us that promise and miracle because it is at that same place that God in His mercy will resurrect that miracle.

For example, when the servants of God under whom we serve in our various churches and fellowships (which are our places of assignment and purpose) minister to us by praying over us, prophesying to us and invoking the miracles of God for us.

We must be careful to remain connected to those servants of God and more so to return to that place of our assignment and purpose where we got that miracle if and when that miracle needs to be resurrected.

5. SHE UNDERSTOOD WHERE THE REAL ANOINTING WAS

When her miracle son died, she did not want to go into details with her husband about it, because she did not want her husband's lack of revelation or insight into the things of God, to interfere with the resurrection power she knew was about to manifest and revive her miracle son. Hence the reason she told her husband *"It is well"*.

2 Kings 4:23 - So he said, "Why are you going to him today? It is neither the New Moon nor the Sabbath." And she said, "It is well."

She went up to Mt. Carmel to get Elisha, meaning that she chose to look up and go up for help signifying her faith and hope instead of going down or looking down in discouragement.

2 Kings 4:25 - And so she departed, and went to the man of God at Mount Carmel. So it was, when the man of God saw her afar off, that he said to his servant Gehazi, "Look, the Shunammite woman!

Gehazi was not enough for her because she wanted the real anointing that could only be found in Elisha and she discerned that the resurrection of her miracle son needed that higher level of power and anointing and not the delegated anointing on Gehazi.

This also reveals a valuable point, that often there are those serving under a servant of God who are supposed to be carrying and operating in the spirit, grace and anointing of that servant of God so as to be able to help the servant of God by ministering to the saints.

This is the principle that Jethro, Moses's father-in-law was trying to instill in him when he advised him to release the spirit that was in him upon his elders so that they could help him to minister to the people.

Exodus 18:19-22 - Listen now to my voice; I will give you counsel, and God will be with you: Stand before God for the people, so that you may bring the difficulties to God. [20] And you shall teach them the statutes and the laws, and show them the way in which they must walk and the work they must do. [21] Moreover you shall select from all the people able men, such as fear God, men of truth, hating covetousness; and place such over them to be rulers of thousands, rulers of hundreds, rulers of fifties, and rulers of tens. [22] And let them judge the people at all times. Then it will be that every great matter they shall bring to you, but every small matter they themselves shall judge. So it will be easier for you, for they will bear the burden with you.

However, there are some who have the **"Gehazi spirit"** meaning that despite sitting and serving under a powerful servant of God their habits and behaviours hinder them from being effective and credible.

6. SHE HAD FAITH AND TRUST IN GOD'S POWER

The **Shunammite woman** had seen God's miraculous power in the birth of her miracle son, so she had faith that the same power of God would resurrect her son. She had no doubt whatsoever that Elisha would be used of God to resurrect her son.

Often even after God has done miraculous things in our lives we soon forget when we encounter a crisis and we begin to see the magnitude of that crisis instead of remembering the power of God.

This is what happened to the children of Israel whenever they encountered a crisis while journeying to the promised land and instead of remembering God's miraculous power at the Red Sea they would panic and lose all faith and trust in God.

Exodus 14:21 - Then Moses stretched out his hand over the sea; and the Lord caused the sea to go back by a strong east wind all that night, and made the sea into dry land, and the waters were divided.

7. SHE WAS OBEDIENT

The **Shunammite woman** was obedient to the leading of the Holy Spirit when she sensed that she should create space and build a room for Elisha. This means that it is not enough to just discern what God wants you to do, the next step of obeying and actually doing that which God wants you to do is even more important.

Sometimes many of us discern and we get the prompting of the Holy Spirit with regard to something God wants us to do but unfortunately, we never get to do it either because we procrastinate instead of promptly obeying.

Sometimes because we start to second guess God and, in the process, we miss the moment or worse still we choose to disobey because whatever the Holy Spirit is prompting us to do sounds too difficult and we are not ready to make the sacrifice.

So, we come up with excuses like "my husband will not agree to this" without realizing that if the prompting and instruction is of God then He will surely align everyone He needs to align in our lives to allow us to obey that instruction.

Her obedience continued to reap benefits for her even years later. A time came after the famine when she encountered Elisha again at the Kings palace and he testified of her generosity which led the King to command his men to restore all her land that had been taken away plus interest and restoration of everything she had lost.

2 Kings 6:5-8 - But as one was cutting down a tree, the iron ax head fell into the water; and he cried out and said, "Alas, master! For it was borrowed." ⁶ So the man of God said, "Where did it fall?"

And he showed him the place. So, he cut off a stick, and threw it in there; and he made the iron float. ⁷ Therefore he said, "Pick it up for yourself." So, he reached out his hand and took it. ⁸ Now the king of Syria was making war against Israel; and he consulted with his servants, saying, "My camp will be in such and such a place."

In short, the Shunammite woman, did something that was so sincere and with a pure heart that caused God to give her a supernatural miracle that she had probably long given up on.

This means that one of the key things that will move us from our distress to our destiny is remaining sensitive to the promptings of the Holy Spirit and to the needs of the servants of God and the work of God. As we sacrificially respond to those needs, God will remember us and do beyond and above our greatest expectations. Miracles will chase us instead of us chasing the miracles.

CHAPTER 7

The Power Of Choice

Your Choices Will Either Keep You in Distress

or Move You into Your Destiny

Chapter Preview

1. **Nehemiah**

    (The Choice To Move From Your Comfort Zone In Order To Rebuild Your Broken Spiritual Walls)

2. **Queen Esther**

    (The Choice to Be a Voice to the Voiceless)

3. **Abigail**

    (The Choice To Shift Allegiances And Loyalties And Align With The Move Of God)

4. **Abraham**

    (The Choice To Obey God Unconditionally And Trust Him Irrevocably)

5. **Naaman**

    (The Choice To Humble Yourself In Order To Lay Hold Of Your Healing)

6. **Peter**

    (The Choice To Arise And Move On From Past Failures)

7. **Gideon**

    (The Choice To Allow God's Strength To Work Through Your Weakness)

8. **Jabez**

   (*The Choice To Rebrand And Expand*)

9. **Woman with issue of Blood**

   (*The Choice To Put Your Destiny Above Your Dignity*)

10. **Blind Bartimaeus**

    (*The Choice To Shout For Your Miracle*)

11. **Daniel**

    (*The Choice To Walk In Righteousness*)

12. **Lot**

    (*The Choice To Disconnect From Your Right Place And Right People*)

13. **Mephibosheth**

    (*The Choice To Arise From Your Crippled State And Embrace God's Favour*)

14. **Paul**

    (*The Choice To Make A Paradigm Shift*)

15. **Rachel**

    (*The Choice To Focus On The Wrong Things*)

16. **Leah**

    (*The Choice To Die To The Approval Of Men*))

17. **Elisha**

    (*The Choice To Discover And Embark On The Purpose For Which You Were Created*)

18. **Elijah**

    (*The Choice To Be God's Remnant*)

19. **Rahab**

   (*The Choice To Make A Radical Relocation And Align Yourself With God And His People*)

20. **Caleb and Joshua**

   (*The Choice To Take God At His Word In Order To Lay Hold Of Your Inheritance*)

21. **The Woman with the Alabastar jar**

   (*The Choice To Put The Cost Of Your Destiny Above The Cost Of Material Substance*)

22. **Samson**

   (*The Choice To Reclaim Your Power And Authority*)

23. **Noah**

   (*The Choice To Put Your Trust In God Above Your Fear Of Ridicule*)

24. **Joseph**

   (*The Choice To Rise Above Past Pain And Betrayal And Forgive Those Who Sought To Kill Your Destiny*)

25. **Job**

   (*The Choice To Refuse To Curse God Even When You Feel He Has Forsaken You*)

26. **Jonah**

   (*The Choice To Resist Or Surrender To The Will Of God*)

27. **Isaac**

   (*The Choice To Sow Abundantly In Your Seasons Of Lack*)

28. Jochebed

(The Choice To Place The Destiny Of Your Child Above Your Own Safety)

29. Hannah

(The Choice To Press And Travail For The Best That God Has For You And To Refuse To Settle For Less)

30. Hezekiah

(The Choice To Reject Death When You Feel That You Have Not Quite Fulfilled Your Purpose)

OPENING REMARKS

Beyond the Biblical characters addressed in the preceding chapters, there are many other characters in the Bible who made certain right critical choices and decisions and took certain steps and actions to move from Distress to Destiny. However, there are also other characters in the Bible, who failed to make the right critical choices and decisions or they made the wrong choices and decisions that caused them to remain in their place of distress and miss entering their place of destiny.

1. NEHEMIAH

(The Choice to Move From Your Comfort Zone in Order to Rebuild Your Broken Spiritual Walls)

Nehemiah reached the point where he was in distress when he heard about the broken walls of Jerusalem. He took the risk to seek favour with the King to go and rebuild the walls of Jerusalem. Nehemiah was able to move his people from a place of distress to destiny by rebuilding the walls, which symbolized the rebuilding, restoration and reestablishment of the place of worship and the repenting by the people in order to rebuild their own broken spiritual walls.

Nehemiah's decision to obey the burden in his heart the broken walls in Jerusalem and his decision to take the necessary actions, despite the fact that he was already in a comfortable prestigious position in the palace as the king's cup bearer.

Often, many are reluctant to move from their comfort zone, good jobs, and positions, wealth and social status, in order to fulfill God's purpose, without realizing that no matter how outwardly successful you may appear (like Nehemiah) unless that success, wealth, status and position is aligned to and within the purpose of God for you then ironically you are actually in a place of distress.

Nehemiah remained focused and refused to be distracted by opposition or sabotage.

Like Nehemiah, your ability to discern the time to rebuild the broken walls of your spiritual life and make a radical choice to do that which promote God's agenda without losing focus is what will move you from distress to destiny.

Nehemiah 1:3-4 *(NKJV) "And they said to me, "The survivors who are left from the captivity in the province are there in great distress and reproach. The wall of Jerusalem is also broken down, and its gates are burned with fire. ⁴ So it was, when I heard these words, that I sat down and wept, and mourned for many days; I was fasting and praying before the God of heaven.*

Nehemiah 2:1-3 (NKJV) *"And it came to pass in the month of Nisan, in the twentieth year of King Artaxerxes, when wine was before him, that I took the wine and gave it to the king. Now I had never been sad in his presence before. ²Therefore the king said to me, "Why is your face sad, since you are not sick? This is nothing but sorrow of heart." So, I became dreadfully afraid, ³and said to the king, "May the king live forever! Why should my face not be sad, when the city, the place of my fathers' tombs, lies waste, and its gates are burned with fire?" ⁴Then the king said to me, "What do you request?"*

Nehemiah 1:4-5 (NKJV) *"So it was, when I heard these words, that I sat down and wept, and mourned for many days; I was fasting and praying before the God of heaven. ⁵ And I said: "I pray, Lord God of heaven, O great and awesome God, You who keep Your covenant and mercy with those who love You and observe Your commandments."*

Nehemiah 4:1-3 (NKJV) *"But it so happened, when Sanballat heard that we were rebuilding the wall, that he was furious and very indignant, and mocked the Jews. ² And he spoke before his brethren* *and the army of Samaria, and said, "What are these feeble Jews doing? Will they fortify themselves? Will they offer sacrifices? Will they complete it in a day? Will they revive the stones from the heaps of rubbish—stones that are burned?"³ Now Tobiah the Ammonite was beside him, and he said, "Whatever they build, if even a fox goes up on it, he will break down their stone wall."*

Nehemiah 4:6 (NKJV) *"⁶ So we built the wall, and the entire wall was joined together up to half its height, for the people had a mind to work."*

Nehemiah 6:15-16 (NKJV) *"15 So the wall was finished on the twenty-fifth day of Elul, in fifty-two days. And it happened, when all our enemies heard of it, and all the nations around us saw these things, that they were very disheartened in their own eyes; for they perceived that this work was done by our God."*

2. QUEEN ESTHER

(The Choice to Be a Voice to the Voiceless)

Queen Esther was in distress when Mordecai her uncle told her of Haman's plot to destroy, kill and annihilate her people (Jewish). She decided to take the risk of her life by seeking favour with the King so as to spare her people. There was a high chance that Esther would face death for approaching the king when the King had not summoned her.

Fortunately, she found favour and the Jewish people were spared and the King ordered that Haman be hang on the same gallows that he had prepared for Mordecai and later the king ordered the destruction of Haman's entire household. The King also mandated Mordecai and Esther to write a decree using his seal and his signet ring.

Esther was able to move her people from distress to their destiny, because she chose to risk her life and speak up for them. Moving from distress to destiny calls for radical action on our part even when the action may be life threatening.

Like Esther when you find yourself in a position of privilege and power (whether it is in your family, corporate organization, church, business empire, government sector etc.) you must use that privilege and power to serve mankind and God's will, otherwise that very place will become a place of distress for you.

Esther 4:6-8 (NKJV) *"⁶ So Hathach went out to Mordecai in the city square that was in front of the king's gate. ⁷ And Mordecai told him all that had happened to him, and the sum of money that Haman had promised to pay into the king's treasuries to destroy the Jews. ⁸ He also gave him a copy of the written decree for their destruction, which was given at Shushan, that he might show it to Esther and explain it to her, and that he might command her to go in to the king to make supplication to him and plead before him for her people."*

Esther 4:10-12 *(NKJV) "¹⁰ Then Esther spoke to Hathach, and gave him a command for Mordecai: ¹¹ "All the king's servants and the people of the king's provinces know that any man or woman who goes into the inner court to the king, who has not been called, he has but one law: put all to death, except the one to whom the king holds out the golden scepter, that he may live. Yet I myself have not been called to go in to the king these thirty days." ¹² So they told Mordecai Esther's words."*

Esther 5:1-3 (NKJV) *"Now it happened on the third day that Esther put on her royal robes and stood in the inner court of the king's palace, across from the king's house, while the king sat on his royal throne in the royal house, facing the entrance of the house. ² So it was, when the king saw Queen Esther standing in the court, that she found favor in his sight, and the king held out to Esther the golden scepter that was in his hand. Then Esther went near and touched the top of the scepter. ³ And the king said to her, "What do you wish, Queen Esther? What is your request? It shall be given to you—up to half the kingdom!"*

Esther. 4:14 (NKJV) *"For if you remain completely silent at this time, relief and deliverance will arise for the Jews from another place, but you and your father's house will perish. Yet who knows whether you have come to the kingdom for such a time as this?"*

Esther 4:16 (NKJV) ¹⁶ *"Go, gather all the Jews who are present in Shushan, and fast for me; neither eat nor drink for three days, night or day. My maids and I will fast likewise. And so, I will go to the king, which is against the law; and if I perish, I perish!"*

Esther 8:7-8 *"⁷ Then King Ahasuerus said to Queen Esther and Mordecai the Jew, "Indeed, I have given Esther the house of Haman, and they have hanged him on the gallows because he tried to lay his hand on the Jews. ⁸You yourselves write a decree concerning the Jews, as you please, in the king's name, and seal it with the king's signet ring; for whatever is written in the king's name and sealed with the king's signet ring no one can revoke."*

3. ABIGAIL

(The Choice to Shift Allegiances and Loyalties and Align with the Move of God)

Abigail was the wife of a wealthy but foolish man called Nabal. We recall that Nabal foolishly rejected and insulted David's request. When Abigail heard of her husband's folly, she hastily decided to do damage control and seek David's forgiveness on behalf of her husband. That way, she spared her husband and her household from David's wrath, and she also prevented David from defiling himself by shedding unnecessary blood.

She discerned that David was God's choice for the new move of Israel at that time and that God's hand was upon David preparing him for the throne. So, Abigail made a prompt decision to accommodate David's request and, in the process, she connected herself to David and thereby moved from her distressful marriage to a marriage with David that was destiny oriented.

Like Abigail, sometimes you may need to discern a defining moment when to make a radical choice and decision and take the necessary steps and actions to shift your allegiance from a place of distress to a place of destiny, whether it is in terms of relationships, business associations and networks or professional partnerships or even fundamental alliances.

1st **Samuel 25:2-3** (NKJV) *"2Now there was a man in Maon whose business was in Carmel, and the man was very rich. He had three thousand sheep and a thousand goats. And he was shearing his sheep in Carmel. 3 The name of the man was Nabal, and the name of his wife Abigail. And she was a woman of good understanding and beautiful appearance; but the man was harsh and evil in his doings. He was of the house of Caleb."*

1 Samuel.25:9-12 (NKJV) *9 So when David's young men came, they spoke to Nabal according to all these words in the name of David, and waited. 10 Then Nabal answered David's servants, and said, "Who is David, and who is the son of Jesse? There are many servants nowadays who break away each one from his master. 11 Shall I then take my bread and my water and my meat that I have killed for my shearers, and give it to men when I do not know where they are from? "12 So David's young men turned on their heels and went back; and they came and told him all these words."*

1 Samuel 25:14-19 (NKJV) *"14 Now one of the young men told Abigail, Nabal's wife, saying, "Look, David sent messengers from the wilderness to greet our master; and he reviled them. 15 But the men were very good* *to us, and we were not hurt, nor did we miss anything as long as we accompanied them, when we were in the fields. [16] They were a wall to us both by night and day, all the time we were with them keeping the sheep. [17] Now therefore, know and consider what you will do, for harm is determined against our master and against all his household. For he is such a scoundrel that one cannot speak to him."[18] Then Abigail made haste and took two hundred loaves of bread, two skins of wine, five sheep already dressed, five seahs of roasted grain, one hundred clusters of raisins, and two hundred cakes of figs, and loaded them on donkeys. [19] And she said to her servants, "Go on before me; see, I am coming after you." But she did not tell her husband Nabal."*

1 Samuel 25:23-25 (NKJV) *"[23] Now when Abigail saw David, she dismounted quickly from the donkey, fell on her face before David, and bowed down to the ground. [24] So she fell at his feet and said: "On me, my lord, on me let this iniquity be! And please let your maidservant speak in your ears, and hear the words of your maidservant. [25] Please, let not my lord regard this scoundrel Nabal. For as his name is, so is he: Nabal is his name, and folly is with him! But I, your maidservant, did not see the young men of my lord whom you sent."*

1 Samuel 25:39 (NKJV) *"[39] So when David heard that Nabal was dead, he said, "Blessed be the Lord, who has pleaded the cause of my reproach from the hand of Nabal, and has kept His servant from evil! For the Lord has returned the wickedness of Nabal on his own head." And David sent and proposed to Abigail, to take her as his wife."*

4. ABRAHAM

(The Choice to Obey God Unconditionally and Trust Him Irrevocably)

Abraham did three things that moved him from his distress to his destiny. **Firstly,** he obeyed God promptly when God instructed him to move away from his father's house in Haran and move to a land that God will show him. Abraham did not need to understand why God wanted him to move because he trusted God enough to believe that the instruction to move from one place to another was ultimately for his own good and for his destiny. Perhaps if Abraham had disobeyed and remained there, he would have found himself in great distress.

Our ability to believe in an all-knowing wise God and to trust that His plans for us are for a hope and a future will enable us to obey His actions promptly without questioning, murmuring or procrastination and thereby move us from our distresses to our destiny.

Secondly, Abraham unlike his wife Sarah made a choice to believe God's promise to bless him with many children and he knew that God would fulfil that promise no matter how long it took. So even though his childlessness caused him distress at times he knew that ultimately God would move him from that distress. In fact, it was his wife Sarah who appears to have mislead him into becoming impatient and birthing an Ishmael otherwise Abraham would have waited patiently.

It is important that we beware of people around us usually those very close to us who may seek to weaken our faith because of the weakness of their own faith and thereby cause us to question and second-guess God's promises of become impatient when they appear to be taking too long.

Thirdly and perhaps the most radical decision and action that Abraham took is when God told him to go sacrifice his son Isaac (which obviously must have caused him some level of distress as this was his only son and the son of promise) but Abraham embarked on obeying that painful instruction without batting an eyelid, again because he did not have to understand God's reasoning suffice, he knew that God would never do anything to harm him or prejudice him. This kind of radical faith, unconditional obedience and irrevocable trust in God was key in ushering Abraham into every promise that God had made to him and more and ultimately to his destiny.

Many of us remain in places of distress whether in terms of our health, relationships, finances and business, career and profession etc. because of our inability and reluctance to operate like Abraham with a radical faith, unconditional obedience and irrevocable trust in God.

Abraham was in distress because of his childlessness and he was both old in age. God had promised Abraham a Nation through his offspring. Abraham choice to believe in God despite the odds, he waited until God honoured his word and blessed them with a son. Abraham's faith helped him move from a place of distress to destiny and he became the father of Nations.

Genesis 16:1-4 (NKJV) *"Now Sarai, Abram's wife, had borne him no children. And she had an Egyptian maidservant whose name was Hagar. ² So Sarai said to Abram, "See now, the Lord has restrained me from bearing children. Please, go in to my maid; perhaps I shall obtain children by her." And Abram heeded the voice of Sarai. ³ Then Sarai, Abram's wife, took Hagar her maid, the Egyptian, and gave her to her husband Abram to be his wife, after Abram had dwelt ten years in the land of Canaan. ⁴ So he went in to Hagar, and she conceived. And when she saw that she had conceived, her mistress became despised in her eyes."*

Genesis 22:1-2 (NKJV) *"Now it came to pass after these things that God tested Abraham, and said to him, "Abraham!" And he said, "Here I am." ² Then He said, "Take now your son, your only son Isaac, whom you love, and go to the land of Moriah, and offer him there as a burnt offering on one of the mountains of which I shall tell you."*

Genesis.15:2 (NKJV) *"But Abram said, "Lord GOD, what will You give me, seeing I go childless, and the heir of my house is Eliezer of Damascus?"*

Genesis 15:4-5 (NKJV) *"⁴ And behold, the word of the LORD came to him, saying, "This one shall not be your heir, but one who will come from your own body shall be your heir." ⁵ Then He brought him outside and said, "Look now toward heaven, and count the stars if you are able to number them." And He said to him, "So shall your descendants be."*

Genesis 21:2 (NKJV) *"2 For Sarah conceived and bore Abraham a son in his old age, at the set time of which God had spoken to him."*

Genesis 12:1-5 - *Now the Lord had said to Abram: "Get out of your country, From your family And from your father's house, To a land that I will show you. ² I will make you a great nation; I will bless you And make your name great; And you shall be a blessing. ³ I will bless those who bless you, And I will curse him who curses you; And in you all the families of the earth shall be blessed." ⁴ So Abram departed as the Lord had spoken to him, and Lot went with him. And Abram was seventy-five years old when he departed from Haran. ⁵ Then Abram took Sarai his wife and Lot his brother's son, and all their possessions that they had gathered, and the people whom they had acquired in Haran, and they departed to go to the land of Canaan. So, they came to the land of Canaan.*

5. NAMAAN

(The Choice To Humble Yourself In Order To Lay Hold Of Your Healing)

Naaman was in distress when he was suffering from leprosy. His maid servant a captive young girl from the land of Israel told her mistress if her master would go to Samaria a prophet in Israel would heal him. He decided to go seek healing from a prophet in Israel.

When he chose to obey the prophet's bizarre instructions by bathing 7 times in River Jordan, he was made whole and therefore he moved from his place of distress towards his destiny. Naaman chose to obey this instruction even though he was risking his reputation and the loss of his credibility in the eyes of those he was leading and even though the advice to obey the prophet was from a mere servant girl.

Like Naaman, moving from our distress to our destiny may require doing what we consider humiliating, embarrassing and a smear on our reputation but provided we close our ears to the opinions of men and open our ears to God's instructions then we will move from our place of distress to destiny, and those who sought to mock us will be shocked at the heights God will propel us to.

God can choose to use even those we least expect in order to move us from distress to destiny, so we must be careful not to despise how God packages His help for us.

2 Kings 5:1-4 (NKJV) *"Now Naaman, commander of the army of the king of Syria, was a great and honorable man in the eyes of his master, because by him the Lord had given victory to Syria. He was also a mighty man of valor, but a leper. ² And the Syrians had gone out on raids, and had brought back captive a young girl from the land of Israel. She waited on Naaman's wife. ³ Then she said to her mistress, "If only my master were with the prophet who is in Samaria! For he would heal him of his leprosy." ⁴ And Naaman went in and told his master, saying, "Thus and thus said the girl who is from the land of Israel."*

2 Kings 5:9-10 (NKJV) *"⁹ Then Naaman went with his horses and chariot, and he stood at the door of Elisha's house. ¹⁰ And Elisha sent a messenger to him, saying, "Go and wash in the Jordan seven times, and your flesh shall be restored to you, and you shall be clean."*

2 Kings 5:13-14 (NKJV) *"13 And his servants came near and spoke to him, and said, "My father, if the prophet had told you to do something great, would you not have done it? How much more then, when he says to you, 'Wash, and be clean'?" 14 So he went down and dipped seven times in the Jordan, according to the saying of the man of God; and his flesh was restored like the flesh of a little child, and he was clean."*

6. PETER

(The Choice to Arise and Move on From Past Failures)

Peter was in distress when he denied Jesus three times. He decided to rise above his weaknesses and preach the gospel of the resurrected Christ on the Pentecost and throughout his life he was able to move from his place of distress to destiny. Peter remembered that Jesus had called him a **"rock"**, so he chose to reject the label of a betrayer and to embrace his true identity in Christ.

Like Peter sometimes we mess big time but provided that we have a heart for destiny deep down a time will always come when we will have a chance to be redeemed from our wrong choices and restored to our path of destiny.

Remembering who we are in Christ and what we were created for will motivate us to arise from our weaknesses, failures and distresses and move on to destiny.

Peter was able to overcome his past mistakes and failures and go on to become one of the most powerful disciples and apostles of Christ.

Luke 22:59 (NKJV) *"59 Then after about an hour had passed, another confidently affirmed, saying, "Surely this fellow also was with Him, for he is a Galilean."*

Mat.26:74-75 (NKJV) *[74] then he began to curse and swear, saying, "I do not know the man!" Immediately a rooster crowed. [75] And Peter remembered the word of Jesus who had said to him, "Before the rooster crows, you will deny me three times." So, he went out and wept bitterly.*

Acts 2:14-17 (NKJV) *But Peter, standing up with the eleven, raised his voice and said to them, "Men of Judea and all who dwell in Jerusalem, let this be known to you, and heed my words. [15] For these are not drunk, as you suppose, since it is only the third hour of the day. [16] But this is what was spoken by the prophet Joel:[17]* 'And it shall come to pass in the last days, says God, That I will pour out of My Spirit on all flesh; Your sons and your daughters shall prophesy, your young men shall see visions, Your old men shall dream dreams."

Acts 5:15 (NKJV) *"so that they brought the sick out into the streets and laid them on beds and couches, that at least the shadow of Peter passing by might fall on some of them."*

7. GIDEON

(The Choice To Allow God's Strength To Work Through Your Weakness)

Gideon was in distress because of the oppression of the Midianite. He chose to listen to the angel of God and followed all instructions given him. He was able to conquer the Midian army and rescue the Jewish people. Therefore, Israel was able to move from Distress to destiny through Gideon's obedience to God's instructions.

Like Gideon we must constantly remember that God's ways are not our ways and that we should not lean on our own understanding, logic and intelligence but rather lean on God's wisdom. Sometimes our education and accumulated knowledge may become a hindrance to our ability to obey God's instructions that appear odd, but we must remember that our own human wisdom is no match to God's wisdom.

1 Corinthians 1:25 (NKJV) *"²⁵Because the foolishness of God is wiser than men, and the weakness of God is stronger than men.*

In addition, we must shed off our negative perceptions of ourselves and believe what God says about us and respond to what He calls us. Gideon's motivation came from God calling him a mighty man of Valor which revoked Gideon's own limitation of self.

Judges 6:12 (NKJV) *"And the Angel of the LORD appeared to him, and said to him, "The LORD is with you, you mighty man of valor!"*

Judges 6:15 (NKJV) *¹⁵ "So he said to Him, "O my Lord, how can I save Israel? Indeed, my clan is the weakest in Manasseh, and I am the least in my father's house."*

Judges 7:4 (NKJV) *"⁴ But the Lord said to Gideon, "The people are still too many; bring them down to the water, and I will test them for you there. Then it will be, that of whom I say to you, 'This one shall go with you,' the same shall go with you; and of whomever I say to you, 'This one shall not go with you,' the same shall not go."*

Judges 7:7 (NKJV) *"⁷ Then the Lord said to Gideon, "By the three hundred men who lapped I will save you, and deliver the Midianites into your hand…"*

Judges 7:13-15 (NKJV) *"¹³ And when Gideon had come, there was a man telling a dream to his companion. He said, "I have had a dream: To my surprise, a loaf of barley bread tumbled into the camp of Midian; it came to a tent and struck it so that it fell and overturned, and the tent collapsed." ¹⁴ Then his companion answered and said, "This is nothing else but the sword of Gideon the son of Joash, a man of Israel! Into his hand God has delivered*

Midian and the whole camp." ¹⁵ And so it was, when Gideon heard the telling of the dream and its interpretation, that he worshiped. He returned to the camp of Israel, and said, "Arise, for the Lord has delivered the camp of Midian into your hand."

Judges 8:22-24 (NKJV) *"²² Then the men of Israel said to Gideon, "Rule over us, both you and your son, and your grandson also; for you have delivered us from the hand of Midian." ²³ But Gideon said to them, "I will not rule over you, nor shall my son rule over you; the Lord shall rule over you." ²⁴ Then Gideon said to them, "I would like to make a request of you, that each of you would give me the earrings from his plunder." For they had golden earrings, because they were Ishmaelites."*

8. JABEZ

(The Choice To Rebrand And Expand)

Jabez was in distress because his mother named him 'Jabez" because she bore him in pain. Jabez decided to call on God so that God would bless and enlarge his territory and keep him from all evil because his name was a hindrance to his blessings and God heard his cry of distress and he was able to move to his place of destiny.

Jabez realized that there is power in a name and that a name can either propel you to destiny or hold you back in distress.

Sometimes we may carry names, stigmas and labels that seek to hold us back in a place of distress but we have a choice to reject or change those names, labels and stigmas and embrace our true identity in Christ which will then propel us to our destiny.

Like Jabez the day we become tired and restless in our place of distress is the day we will break out of it by making a fervent desperate prayer for a new name and breaking of limitations around us.

1 Chronicles 4:9-10 (NKJV) *"⁹ Now Jabez was more honorable than his brothers, and his mother called his name Jabez, saying, "Because I bore him in pain." ¹⁰ And Jabez called on the God of Israel saying, "Oh, that You would bless me indeed, and enlarge my territory, that Your hand would be with me, and that You would keep me from evil, that I may not cause pain!" So, God granted him what he requested."*

9. THE WOMAN WITH THE ISSUE OF BLOOD

(The Choice To Put Your Destiny Above Your Dignity)

This woman suffered many distresses from seeing many physicians and her condition worsened. She was considered unclean. Physically, she was deficient because of the loss of blood, and she was financially drained. However, she moved from distress to destiny when she decided to risk and touch the hem of Jesus' garment and she was completely healed. Her desperation birthed a radical faith.

Like the woman with the issue of blood when we put aside our pride, dignity and the fakeness of man's protocol, we will break out of our distress to destiny. Until the day your distress becomes unbearable you will continue to wallow in stress.

Mark 5:25-26 (NKJV) *"²⁵ Now a certain woman had a flow of blood for twelve years, ²⁶ and had suffered many things from many physicians. She had spent all that she had and was no better, but rather grew worse."*

Mark 5:27-29 (NKJV) *"²⁷ When she heard about Jesus, she came behind Him in the crowd and touched His garment. ²⁸ For she said, "If only I may touch His clothes, I shall be made well."²⁹ Immediately the fountain of her blood was dried up, and she felt in her body that she was healed of the affliction."*

10. BLIND BARTIMAEUS

(*The Choice To Shout For Your Miracle*)

Blind Bartimaeus was in distress as he was blind and desired to see. He made the choice to cry loudly to Jesus for healing even when he was commanded to shut up. He cried louder and Jesus healed him. He was able to move from his place of distress to destiny. Blind Bartimaeus reminds us that being handicapped in one area of our lives (in this case sight and vision) forces us to appreciate and use the other aspects of our life that are not handicapped (in this case the words of your mouth).

If we want to get out of our distress we must have the necessary passion, desperation, stubbornness and urgency like blind Bartimaeus, because only you, know the pain and agony of your distress and only you possess the power of choice to escape it. Moving from distress to destiny is a very personal responsibility and like blind Bartimaeus, you must not allow people to hinder you.

Mark 10:46-47 (NKJV) *"[46] Now they came to Jericho. As He went out of Jericho with His disciples and a great multitude, blind Bartimaeus, the son of Timaeus, sat by the road begging. [47] And when he heard that it was Jesus of Nazareth, he began to cry out and say, "Jesus, Son of David, have mercy on me!"*

Mark 10:48 (NKJV) *"[48] Then many warned him to be quiet; but he cried out all the more, "Son of David, have mercy on me!"*

Mark 10:52 (NKJV) *[52] Then Jesus said to him, "Go your way; your faith has [h]made you well." And immediately he received his sight and followed Jesus on the road."*

11. DANIEL

(*The Choice To Walk In Righteousness*)

Daniel was in distress when his colleagues were jealous of his promotion and trapped him through his Worship of God. Daniel decided not to compromise his Worship and he was thrown in the den of lions.

However, God saved him by closing the lion's mouth. His worship and faithfulness to God made him to move from his place of distress to destiny because a decree was written that none other than the God of Daniel was to be worshipped. Daniel's righteousness was a powerful testimony that impacted even the king who was an unbeliever and it earned him respect and honour even from those who did not worship his God and essentially moved him from the distress of persecution to a place of fulfilling destiny.

Like Daniel, our integrity and choice to live God's way, is a powerful vehicle in moving us from a place of distress (namely the fiery furnaces and the lion's den) to our place of destiny as advisors and counsellors to kings and presidents. The choice to walk righteously therefore without compromise no matter how difficult our circumstances is powerful in propelling us to destiny.

Daniel 1:8 (NKJV) *"But Daniel purposed in his heart that he would not defile himself with the portion of the king's delicacies, nor with the wine which he drank; therefore, he requested of the chief of the eunuchs that he might not defile himself."*

Dan 6:3-4 (NKJV) *"Then this Daniel distinguished himself above the governors and satraps, because an excellent spirit was in him; and the king gave thought to setting him over the whole realm. [4] So the governors and satraps sought to find some charge against Daniel concerning the kingdom; but they could find no charge or fault,* *because he was faithful; nor was there any error or fault found in him."*

Dan 6:11-12 (NKJV) *¹¹ Then these men assembled and found Daniel praying and making supplication before his God. ¹² And they went before the king, and spoke concerning the king's decree: "Have you not signed a decree that every man who petitions any god or man within thirty days, except you, O king, shall be cast into the den of lions?..."*

Dan 6:14-15 (NKJV) *"¹⁴ And the king, when he heard these words, was greatly displeased with himself, and set his heart on Daniel to deliver him; and he labored till the going down of the sun to deliver him. ¹⁵ Then these men approached the king, and said to the king, "Know, O king, that it is the law of the Medes and Persians that no decree or statute which the king establishes may be changed."*

Dan 6:16-17 (NKJV) *"¹⁶ So the king gave the command, and they brought Daniel and cast him into the den of lions. But the king spoke, saying to Daniel, "Your God, whom you serve continually, He will deliver you." ¹⁷ Then a stone was brought and laid on the mouth of the den, and the king sealed it with his own signet ring and with the signets of his lords, that the purpose concerning Daniel might not be changed."*

Dan 6:19-23 (NKJV) *"¹⁹ Then the king arose very early in the morning and went in haste to the den of lions. ²⁰ And when he came to the den, he cried out with a lamenting voice to Daniel. The king spoke, saying to Daniel, A Daniel, servant of the living God, has your God, whom you serve continually, been able to deliver you from the lions? ²¹ Then Daniel said to the king, TO king, live forever! ²² My God sent His angel and shut the lions' mouths, so that they have not hurt me, because I was found innocent before Him; and also, O king, I have done no wrong before you. ²³ Now the king was exceedingly glad for him, and commanded that they should take Daniel up out of the den.*

So, Daniel was taken up out of the den, and no injury whatever was found on him, because he believed in his God."

12. LOT

(The Choice To Disconnect From Your Right Place And Right People)

Lot was Abraham's nephew, and he enjoyed the spiritual fatherhood and mentorship from Abraham, he also enjoyed the protection, provision and privileges that came by virtue of his association with such a noble, wealthy, statesman like Abraham. To that extent we can say that he was rightly positioned and rightly connected i.e., he was with the right people at the right place, so that in time he would have definitely progressed to enter his destiny.

However, Lot made a critical wrong choice and decision by disconnecting from his uncle Abraham and seeking to go solo perhaps because he was self-deceived and deluded into thinking that he had matured enough to stand on his own without protection, cover and mentorship of Abraham.

The second critical wrong choice that Lot made was dishonouring his uncle Abraham (who as stated above, represented his spiritual father and mentor) by daring to choose the most fertile land when they decided to divide and apportion the properties and assets and go their separate ways.

Lot eventually ended up settling in a place of distress in Sodom, and his life never quite stabilised and it would be true to say that he more or less aborted his destiny.

This is the problem with many people today, who rush in haste to claim their independence when they come into a little wealth, influence or success and they make the critical mistake of disconnecting from their set man of God and from their destiny relationships. In the process they also dislocate themselves from their right place of assignment and purpose, sphere/sector where God had ordained them to be.

Identifying, connecting and remaining connected in the right relationships plus the locating and positioning yourself in your right place where you will fulfil your purpose are crucial fundamentals in moving from distress to destiny.

Genesis 13:8-11 (NKJV) *"⁸ So Abram said to Lot, "Please let there be no strife between you and me, and between my herdsmen and your herdsmen; for we are brethren. ⁹ Is not the whole land before you? Please separate from me. If you take the left, then I will go to the right; or, if you go to the right, then I will go to the left."*

¹⁰ And Lot lifted his eyes and saw all the plain of Jordan, that it was well watered everywhere (before the Lord destroyed Sodom and Gomorrah) like the garden of the Lord, like the land of Egypt as you go toward Zoar. ¹¹ Then Lot chose for himself all the plain of Jordan, and Lot journeyed east. And they separated from each other."

Genesis 19:3-5 (NKJV) *"³ But he insisted strongly; so, they turned in to him and entered his house. Then he made them a feast, and baked unleavened bread, and they ate. ⁴ Now before they lay down, the men of the city, the men of Sodom, both old and young, all the people from every quarter, surrounded the house. ⁵ And they called to Lot and said to him, "Where are the men who came to you tonight? Bring them out to us that we may know them carnally."*

Genesis 19:9-10 (NKJV) *"⁹ And they said, "Stand back!" Then they said, "This one came in to stay here, and he keeps acting as a judge; now we will deal worse with you than with them." So, they pressed hard against the man Lot, and came near to break down the door. ¹⁰ But the men reached out their hands and pulled Lot into the house with them, and shut the door."*

Genesis 19:16-17 (NKJV) *"¹⁶ And while he lingered, the men took hold of his hand, his wife's hand, and the hands of his two daughters, the Lord being merciful to him, and they brought him out and set him outside the city. ¹⁷ So it came to pass, when they had brought them outside, that he said, "Escape for your life! Do not look behind you nor stay anywhere in the plain. Escape to the mountains, lest you be destroyed."*

Genesis 19:23-26 (NKJV) *"²³ By the time Lot reached Zoar, the sun had risen over the land. ²⁴ Then the Lord rained down burning sulfur on Sodom and Gomorrah—from the Lord out of the heavens. ²⁵ Thus he overthrew those cities and the entire plain, destroying all those living in the cities—and also the vegetation in the land. ²⁶ But Lot's wife looked back, and she became a pillar of salt."*

13. MEPHIBOSHETH

(The Choice to Arise From Your Crippled State and Embrace God's Favour)

Mephibosheth was the son of Jonathan and the grandson of King Saul, who found himself in a place of distress after the deaths of Saul and Jonathan. Mephibosheth's nurse took him and fled in panic and in haste dropped Mephibosheth and he became crippled.

He continued to dwell in the place of distress for several years and he almost gave up but by the grace of God and because of the covenant that David had made with Mephibosheth's father (Jonathan) a day came when David remembered that covenant and inquired after Mephibosheth and commanded that he be brought to the palace immediately and sit and dine at the King's table for the rest of his life.

In essence Mephibopsheth's moving from the place of distress to a place of destiny was not as a result of something good that he had done but it was as a result of something that his father had done years before (namely helping David when David was in distress which led to the covenant between him and David which was now benefitting his son Mephibosheth)

This story demonstrates the power of divine covenant relationships between you and others or even between your fathers (parent) and others. It also shows the power that those divine covenant relationships have in moving you from a place of distress to destiny.

2nd **Samuel 9:3(d) (NKJV)** *"And Ziba said to the king, "There is still a son of Jonathan who is lame in his feet."*

2nd **Samuel 9:7-8 "(NKJV)** *"So David said to him, "Do not fear, for I will surely show you kindness for Jonathan your father's sake, and will restore to you all the land of Saul your grandfather; and you shall eat bread at my table continually. Then he bowed himself, and said, "What is your servant, that you should look upon such a dead dog as I?"*

2nd **Samuel 9:9-10 (NKJV)** *"And the king called to Ziba, Saul's servant, and said to him, "I have given to your master's son all that belonged to Saul and to all his house. You therefore, and your sons and your servants, shall work the land for him, and you shall bring in the harvest, that your master's son may have food to eat. But Mephibosheth your master's son shall eat bread at my table always." Now Ziba had fifteen sons and twenty servants."*

14. PAUL

(The Choice to Make a Paradigm Shift)

We find Paul the Apostle throughout the New Testament and our first encounter with him is when he was still Saul a non-believer persecuting Christians. And to that extent was in a place of distress because even though he was deluded into thinking he was in the right path; he was desperately lost without direction because he had not yet discovered his true purpose and his God-given assignment and so the enemy was using him to accomplish hurt on the people and the work of God. However, God in his mercies stepped into Saul's life and radically transformed him into Paul one of the greatest Apostles of our time who went on to fulfil destiny by spreading the gospel of Jesus Christ worldwide.

Paul's decision to embrace his **"Damascus moment"** and obediently embrace his transformation was critical in moving him from his distress to his destiny.

Sometimes God desires to radically transform us so as to move us from our place of distress to our place of destiny, but many of us sadly miss that defining moment by either not recognizing it or by ignoring it, or by totally rejecting it.

Your Moving from distress to destiny will require you to be spiritually alert and sensitive to the moving of God.

Acts 9:1-2 (NKJV) *"Then Saul, still breathing threats and murder against the disciples of the Lord, went to the high priest ² and asked letters from him to the synagogues of Damascus, so that if he found any who were of the Way, whether men or women, he might bring them bound to Jerusalem."*

Acts 9:3-6 (NKJV) *"³ As he journeyed, he came near Damascus, and suddenly a light shone around him from heaven. ⁴ Then he fell to the ground, and heard a voice saying to him, "Saul, Saul, why are you persecuting Me?"⁵ And he said, "Who are You, Lord?" Then the Lord said, "I am Jesus, whom you are persecuting. [a]It is hard for you to kick against the goads." ⁶ So he, trembling and astonished, said, "Lord, what do You want me to do?..."*

2ⁿᵈ Cor.11:23 (NKJV) *"²³ Are they ministers of Christ? I speak as a fool—I am more: in labors more abundant, in stripes above measure, in prisons more frequently, in deaths often. ²⁴ From the Jews five times I received forty stripes minus one. ²⁵ Three times I was beaten with rods; once I was stoned; three times I was shipwrecked; a night and a day I have been in the deep; ²⁶ in journeys often, in perils of waters, in perils of robbers, in perils of my own countrymen, in perils of the Gentiles, in perils in the city, in perils in the wilderness, in perils in the sea, in perils among false brethren; ²⁷ in weariness and toil, in sleeplessness often, in hunger and thirst, in fastings often, in cold and nakedness— ²⁸ besides the other things, what comes upon me daily: my deep concern for all the churches. ²⁹ Who is weak, and I am not weak? Who is made to stumble, and I do not burn with indignation?*

Acts 28:10 (NKJV)*" They also honored us in many ways; and when we departed, they provided such things as were necessary"*

2 Tim.1:8-9 (NKJV) *"⁸ Therefore do not be ashamed of the testimony of our Lord, nor of me His prisoner, but share with me in the sufferings for the gospel according to the power of God, ⁹ who has saved us and called us with a holy calling, not according to our works, but according to His own purpose and grace which was given to us in Christ Jesus before time began."*

15. RACHEL

(The Choice to Focus on the Wrong Things)

Rachel was the beauty queen daughter of Laban and the love of Jacob's life. Jacob eventually married her after labouring for 14 years (when his uncle Laban deceived him). Rachel found herself in the place of distress when she failed to conceive and bear children for Jacob. She probably thought that her beauty was sufficient or that Jacob's obsessive love for her would automatically break her barrenness, but it did not. Fortunately, and by the grace of God she did eventually bear children. However, her unhealthy competition with her sister Leah made her lose focus on what was important.

Rachel's choice and decision to continue holding on to idol gods from her father's household ultimately hindered her from entering the place of destiny where Jacob was leading his family after they escaped from uncle Laban.

We often focus on the wrong things in our lives like physical beauty, material substance and wealth, which become idols and they take the place of God in our lives and hence we fail to move from distress to destiny.

Rachel's obsession with idol gods despite the fact that she was a believer shows that she was mixing idolatry with the worship of the true God and thereby walking in double mindedness.

As believers when we step out and seek help from witchcraft, divination and sorcery yet we continue to purport to worship the true God, then like Rachel we will remain and die in the place of distress without entering destiny.

Genesis 29:25 (NKJV*)* ***"***25 *So it came to pass in the morning, that behold, it was Leah. And he said to Laban, "What is this you have done to me? Was it not for Rachel that I served you? Why then have you deceived me?"*

Genesis 31:19 (NKJV) *"Now Laban had gone to shear his sheep, and Rachel had stolen the household idols that were her father's."*

Genesis 29:17-18 (NKJV) *"*17*...but Rachel was beautiful of form and appearance.* 18 *Now Jacob loved Rachel; so, he said, "I will serve you seven years for Rachel your younger daughter."*

Genesis 30:1 (NKJV) *"Now when Rachel saw that she bore Jacob no children, Rachel envied her sister, and said to Jacob, "Give me children, or else I die!"*

Genesis 30:22 (NKJV) *"Then God remembered Rachel, and God listened to her and opened her womb. ²³ And she conceived and bore a son, and said, "God has taken away my reproach."*

16. LEAH

(The Choice to Die to the Approval of Men)

Leah was Laban's other less attractive daughter whom he deceived Jacob with. Leah found herself in the place of distress when she realised that Jacob did not love her and he would never love her. She continued to increase her distress by bearing many children with the agenda of winning Jacob's heart and by engaging in a sisterly competition with Rachel.

However, and fortunately, a time came when Leah made a critical turning point in her life when she stopped trying to please man. and instead decided to praise God and give Him the glory. She named her son **Judah** (meaning praise) who went on to become one of the twelve tribes of Israel. To that extent, Leah made a deliberate and intentional choice to come out of her place of distress to her place of destiny.

We often make the mistake of trying to please people and seek their approval and we become bound by other people's opinion of us and we allow that to define us which spins us into an identity crisis.

For a long-time Leah, had erroneously allowed Jacob's love or absence of it to define her and she had also allowed her motherhood to define her without realizing that she was more than all those things and that her true defining and identity could only come from the true God.

In order to move from our places of distress to our places of destiny, we must (like Leah) realize what should and should not define us. We must also die to praises, opinions, and approval of others, and we must reject every negative stigma, wrong label and wrong identity that people may seek to impose upon us.

Genesis 29:16-17 (NKJV) *"¹⁶ Now Laban had two daughters: the name of the elder was Leah, ¹⁷ Leah's eyes were delicate…"*

Genesis 29:31-32;35 (NKJV) *"³¹ When the Lord saw that Leah was unloved, He opened her womb; but Rachel was barren. ³² So Leah conceived and bore a son, and she called his name Reuben; for she said, "The Lord has surely looked on my affliction. Now therefore, my husband will love me…³⁵And she conceived again and bore a son, and said, "Now I will praise the LORD." Therefore, she called his name Judah. Then she stopped bearing."*

Genesis 30:9-11 (NKJV) *"⁹ When Leah saw that she had stopped bearing, she took Zilpah her maid and gave her to Jacob as wife. ¹⁰ And Leah's maid Zilpah bore Jacob a son. ¹¹ Then Leah said, "A troop comes!" So, she called his name Gad."*

17. ELISHA

(The Choice to Discover and Embark on the Purpose for Which You Were Created)

Elisha was the faithful follower and protégé of the great prophet Elijah. He found himself in the place of distress, when he was taking care of his father's oxen which were not his God-ordained assignment or purpose and he was definitely not in his right place.

Elisha made a critical choice and decision to forsake all that he had been doing (which was not aligned to his destiny) and followed Elijah the prophet. In doing so he put in motion his moving from distress to destiny.

Elisha's faithfulness in following and serving Elijah in and out of Season through all the difficult and hard times without turning back earned him the double portion mantle from Elijah.

Our decision and choice to serve and remain connected to our set man of God is crucial in our moving from distress to destiny because of the crucial role that such servants of God have in our lives.

1 Kings 19:20 (NKJV) *"And he left the oxen and ran after Elijah, and said, "Please let me kiss my father and my mother, and then I will follow you." And he said to him, "Go back again, for what have I done to you?"*

2 Kings 2:9-10 (NKJV) *"9 And so it was, when they had crossed over, that Elijah said to Elisha, "Ask! What may I do for you, before I am taken away from you?" Elisha said, "Please let a double portion of your spirit be upon me. 10 So he said, "You have asked a hard thing. Nevertheless, if you see me when I am taken from you, it shall be so for you; but if not, it shall not be so."*

2 Kings 4:38-41 (NKJV) *"38 And Elisha returned to Gilgal, and there was a famine in the land. Now the sons of the prophets were sitting before him; and he said to his servant, "Put on the large pot, and boil stew for the sons of the prophets." 39 So one went out into the field to gather herbs, and found a wild vine, and gathered from it a lapful of wild gourds, and came and sliced them into the pot of stew, though they did not know what they were. 40 Then they served it to the men to eat. Now it happened, as they were eating the stew, that they cried out and said, "Man of God, there is death in the pot!" And they could not eat it. 41 So he said, "Then bring some flour." And he put it into the pot, and said, "Serve it to the people, that they may eat." And there was nothing harmful in the pot."*

18. ELIJAH

(*The Choice To Be God's Remnant*)

Elijah was a great prophet who God used greatly in eradicating idol worship in Israel, by pulling down the altars of Baal and re-establishing the altar of the true God.

However, despite his victorious accomplishments, Elijah found himself in a place of distress when Jezebel swore to eliminate him and he temporarily forgot the power of his God that he had just witnessed at Mt. Carmel, by thinking that Jezebel was more powerful than God. God had to remind Elijah of this and shake him out of his apathy and self-pity.

This is the mistake many of us make especially where the persecution, oppression and opposition continues for a long time in our lives and we come to a point in our lives when we despair and lose hope, instead of trusting in the knowledge that God is more powerful than any persecution, oppression and opposition we may face. Self-pity and victim syndrome can never move us from distress, but courage and faith will.

However, when we come to the revelation of God's power, and we arise like Elijah from our place of distress and choose to trust in God's power to protect us, and we continue to obey and serve God irrespective, then we are in the process of moving from that place of distress to a place of destiny.

1st **Kings 17:2-5 (NKJV)** *"2 Then the word of the Lord came to him, saying, 3 "Get away from here and turn eastward, and hide by the Brook Cherith, which flows into the Jordan. 4 And it will be that you shall drink from the brook, and I have commanded the ravens to feed you there." 5 So he went and did according to the word of the Lord, for he went and stayed by the Brook Cherith, which flows* *into the Jordan. ⁶ The ravens brought him bread and meat in the morning, and bread and meat in the evening; and he drank from the brook."*

1 Kings 19:1-4 (NKJV) *"And Ahab told Jezebel all that Elijah had done, also how he had executed all the prophets with the sword. ² Then Jezebel sent a messenger to Elijah, saying, "So let the gods do to me, and more also, if I do not make your life as the life of one of them by tomorrow about this time." ³ And when he saw that, he arose and ran for his life, and went to Beersheba, which belongs to Judah, and left his servant there. ⁴ But he himself went a day's journey into the wilderness, and came and sat down under a broom tree. And he prayed that he might die, and said, "It is enough! Now, Lord, take my life, for I am no better than my fathers!"*

1 Kings 19:10 (NKJV) *"¹⁰ So he said, "I have been very zealous for the Lord God of hosts; for the children of Israel have forsaken Your covenant, torn down Your altars, and killed Your prophets with the sword. I alone am left; and they seek to take my life."*

1 Kings 18:36-39 (NKJV) *"³⁶ And it came to pass, at the time of the offering of the evening sacrifice, that Elijah the prophet came near and said, "Lord God of Abraham, Isaac, and Israel, let it be known this day that You are God in Israel and I am Your servant, and that I have done all these things at Your word. ³⁷ Hear me, O Lord, hear me, that this people may know that You are the Lord God, and that You have turned their hearts back to You again." ³⁸ Then the fire of the Lord fell and consumed the burnt sacrifice, and the wood and the stones and the dust, and it licked up the water that was in the trench. ³⁹ Now when all the people saw it, they fell on their faces; and they said, "The Lord, He is God! The Lord, He is God!"*

1st **Kings 19:16 (NKJV)** *"Also you shall anoint Jehu the son of Nimshi as king over Israel. And Elisha the son of Shaphat of Abel Meholah you shall anoint as prophet in your place."*

19. RAHAB

(The Choice to Make a Radical Relocation and Align Yourself With God and His People)

Rahab was a prostitute whose house was on top of the city walls of Jericho, and even though she operated a lucrative business, deep down she must have felt unfulfilled because when a day came and she had an opportunity to help the men of God who had come as spies, she did so with the intention of connecting herself with those men and to their God and thereby disconnecting herself from the place and lifestyle of distress.

This radical and risky choice and decision that Rahab made ultimately propelled her into her place of destiny and earned her a place in the lineage and genealogy of Jesus Christ.

Sometimes we know that the place we are at either in our career, business enterprise, profession, ministry etc. is a place of distress and our lifestyle falls short of what we know deep down we have been called into our ability to recognise and step into defining moments where an opportunity arises for us to relocate from that place of distress to a place of destiny is what makes us destiny people.

In addition, the ability to take whatever risks and radical steps are needed for us to make that crucial transition.

Joshua 2:1 (NKJV) *"¹ Now Joshua the son of Nun sent out two men from Acacia Grove to spy secretly, saying, "Go, view the land, especially Jericho." So they went, and came to the house of a harlot named Rahab, and lodged there."*

Joshua 2:4-5 (NKJV) *⁴ Then the woman took the two men and hid them. So, she said, "Yes, the men came to me, but I did not know where they were from. ⁵ And it happened as the gate was being shut, when it was dark, that the men went out. Where the men went, I do not know; pursue them quickly, for you may overtake them."*

Joshua 2:12-13 (NKJV) *"12 Now therefore, I beg you, swear to me by the Lord, since I have shown you kindness, that you also will show kindness to my father's house, and give me a true token, ¹³ and spare my father, my mother, my brothers, my sisters, and all that they have, and deliver our lives from death."*

Joshua 6:25 (NKJV) *"And Joshua spared Rahab the harlot, her father's household, and all that she had. So, she dwells in Israel to this day, because she hid the messengers whom Joshua sent to spy out Jericho."*

Matthew 1:5-6 (NKJV) *"⁵ Salmon begot Boaz by Rahab, Boaz begot Obed by Ruth, Obed begot Jesse, ⁶ and Jesse begot David the king..."*

Matthew 1:17 (NKJV) *"¹⁷ So all the generations from Abraham to David are fourteen generations, from David until the captivity in Babylon are fourteen generations, and from the captivity in Babylon until the Christ are fourteen generations."*

20. CALEB AND JOSHUA

(The Choice to Take God at His Word in Order to Lay Hold of Your Inheritance)

Caleb and Joshua were the faithful followers of Moses and the only two spies who had faith and trust in God's promises about the Promised Land, and in Moses' ability to usher them there.

It was their decision to trust in the prophetic promise despite the giants and the contrary circumstances, that moved them from their distress in Egypt and into their inheritance in the Promised Land.

When God steps in to deliver us from our places of oppression and bondage and from our distress and he promises us an expected end with a future and a hope, it is our choice to have faith and trust in Him (despite what we may encounter along the way) that establishes us in those promises and in our destiny.

Numbers 13:30 (NKJV) *"³⁰ Then Caleb quieted the people before Moses, and said, "Let us go up at once and take possession, for we are well able to overcome it."*

Numbers 14: 6-9 (NKJV) *"⁶ But Joshua the son of Nun and Caleb the son of Jephunneh, who were among those who had spied out the land, tore their clothes; ⁷ and they spoke to all the congregation of the children of Israel, saying: "The land we passed through to spy out is an exceedingly good land. ⁸ If the Lord delights in us, then He will bring us into this land and give it to us, 'a land which flows with milk and honey.' ⁹ Only do not rebel against the Lord, nor fear the people of the land, for they are our bread; their protection has departed from them, and the Lord is with us. Do not fear them."*

Joshua 14:6 (NKJV) *"⁶ Then the children of Judah came to Joshua in Gilgal. And Caleb the son of Jephunneh the Kenizzite said to him: "You know the word which the Lord said to Moses the man of God concerning you and me in Kadesh Barnea."*

Joshua 14: 12-13 (NKJV) *"¹² Now therefore, give me this mountain of which the Lord spoke in that day; for you heard in that day how the Anakim were there, and that the cities were great and fortified. It may be that the Lord will be with me, and I shall be able to drive them out as the Lord said." ¹³ And Joshua blessed him, and gave Hebron to Caleb the son of Jephunneh as an inheritance."*

21. THE WOMAN WITH THE ALABASTAR JAR

(The Choice to Put the Cost of Your Destiny Above the Cost of Material Substance)

This woman found herself in distress because of her prostitute lifestyle that made her despicable to her people. However, a time came when she made a radical choice and decision to turn her life around and embrace what she was born for. Her radical encounter with Jesus and her stubborn tenacious resolve to break all protocol and receive a transformation is what moved her from her distress to destiny.

Recognizing that we are in distress and acknowledging our need for a radical touch and transformation from God is commendable enough, but it is our radical choice and decision to take the necessary action (no matter how offensive it may be to those around us) that ultimately removes us from our distress to our destiny.

Luke 7:37-39 (NKJV) *"37 And behold, a woman in the city who was a sinner, when she knew that Jesus sat at the table in the Pharisee's house, brought an alabaster flask of fragrant oil, 38 and stood at His feet behind Him weeping; and she began to wash His feet with her tears, and wiped them with the hair of her head; and she kissed His feet and anointed them with the fragrant oil. 39 Now when the Pharisee who had invited Him saw this, he spoke to himself, saying, "This Man, if He were a prophet, would know who and what manner of woman this is who is touching Him, for she is a sinner."*

Luke 7:44-47 (NKJV) *"44 Then he turned toward the woman and said to Simon, "Do you see this woman? I came into your house. You did not give me any water for my feet, but she wet my feet with her tears and wiped them with her hair. 45 You did not give me a kiss, but this woman, from the time I entered, has not stopped kissing my feet. 46 You did not put oil on my head, but she has* *poured perfume on my feet. [47] Therefore, I tell you, her many sins have been forgiven—as her great love has shown. But whoever has been forgiven little loves little."*

22. SAMSON

(The Choice to Reclaim Your Power and Authority)

Samson was an Israelite who was supposed to follow the proscriptions of Nazarite life, which included neither drinking nor trimming his locks. He was man of tremendous strength. However, a time came when he deviated from the plan and purposes of God for his life and he disobediently went down from his position of power and authority into the enemy's territory where he prejudiced his power and authority and connected himself to people who God had commanded him to overpower and rule over. He also engaged in an immoral lifestyle thereby defiling himself contrary to God's instructions to maintain purity as a special vessel of God.

Samson found himself in a place of distress when he was deceived to compromise his God-given strength and anointing and his enemies blinded him and took him captive.

Fortunately, after realizing his blunder Samson remembered who he was and who God had created him to be and that revelation in itself, is what gave him the courage to summon himself and destroy his enemies.

Sometimes we may mess and come out of the will God and thereby compromise and threaten our destiny because we have forgotten our identity and position in God but we serve a merciful God and when we do come to that revelation of who we are and what God has deposited in us then we will arise and overcome.

Disengaging ourselves from our ordained purpose and depositioning ourselves from our right place of purpose and assignment will always take us down a very slippery path into a place of distress and defeat.

God in His wisdom cautions and forbids us from connecting to people who He knows will derail us from our destiny, so when we disobey God, we essentially end up in distress.

Judges 16:1-2 (NKJV) *"Now Samson went to Gaza and saw a harlot there, and went in to her. ² When the Gazites were told, "Samson has come here!" they surrounded the place and lay in wait for him all night at the gate of the city. They were quiet all night, saying, "In the morning, when it is daylight, we will kill him."*

Judges 16:15-20 (NKJV) *"¹⁵ Then she said to him, "How can you say, 'I love you,' when your heart is not with me? You have mocked me these three times, and have not told me where your great strength lies." ¹⁶ And it came to pass, when she pestered him daily with her words and pressed him, so that his soul was vexed to death, ¹⁷ that he told her all his heart, and said to her, "No razor has ever come upon my head, for I have been a Nazirite to God from my mother's womb. If I am shaven, then my strength will leave me, and I shall become weak, and be like any other man."¹⁸ When Delilah saw that he had told her all his heart, she sent and called for the lords of the Philistines, saying, "Come up once more, for he has told me all his heart." So the lords of the Philistines came up to her and brought the money in their hand. ¹⁹ Then she lulled him to sleep on her knees, and called for a man and had him shave off the seven locks of his head. Then she began to torment him, and his strength left him. ²⁰ And she said, "The Philistines are upon you, Samson!" So he awoke from his sleep, and said, "I will go out as before, at other times, and shake myself free!" But he did not know that the Lord had departed from him."*

Judges 16:21 (NKJV) *"Then the Philistines took him and put out his eyes, and brought him down to Gaza. They bound him with bronze fetters, and he became a grinder in the prison."*

Judges 16:28-30 (NKJV) *"Then Samson called to the LORD, saying, "O Lord GOD, remember me, I pray! Strengthen me, I pray, just this once, O God, that I may with one blow take vengeance on the Philistines for my two eyes! And Samson took hold of the two middle pillars which supported the temple, and he braced himself against them, one on his right and the other on his left. Then Samson said, "Let me die with the Philistines!" And he pushed with all his might, and the temple fell on the lords and all the people who were in it. So, the dead that he killed at his death were more than he had killed in his life."*

23. NOAH

(The Choice to Put Your Trust in God Above Your Fear of Ridicule)

When God beheld the corruption of the earth and determined to destroy it, he gave Noah divine warning of the impending disaster and made a covenant with him, promising to save him and his family. Noah could have remained in a place of distress and perished together with the other wicked people but he made a radical choice and decision to obey God's instructions.

When God instructed Noah to build an arch to salvage his family from the flood. Noah chose to trust and obey, even though the instructions did not initially make sense and despite the mockery, taunting and ridicule that he had to endure from the people.

Sometimes moving from a place of distress will require us to obey radical instructions from God that makes us look ridiculous, mentally deranged and we even lose credibility in the eyes of those around us. Yet when we are sensitive to the voice of God, we will shut out all other negative voices and ultimately move from distress to destiny.

All those who mocked Noah and hardened their hearts against God's warnings must have got such a shock and must have deeply regretted their hardness and rebellion when the flood came and it was too late for them to enter the Ark with Noah.

Noah and his family escaped distress and entered their destiny.

Genesis 6:5-8 (NKJV) *"⁵ Then the Lord saw that the wickedness of man was great in the earth, and that every intent of the thoughts of his heart was only evil continually. ⁶ And the Lord was sorry that He had made man on the earth, and He was grieved in His heart. ⁷ So the Lord said, "I will destroy man whom I have created from the face of the earth, both man and beast, creeping thing and birds of the air, for I am sorry that I have made them." ⁸ But Noah found grace in the eyes of the Lord."*

Genesis 6:12-14 (NKJV) *"¹² So God looked upon the earth, and indeed it was corrupt; for all flesh had corrupted their way on the earth. ¹³ And God said to Noah, "The end of all flesh has come before Me, for the earth is filled with violence through them; and behold, I will destroy them with the earth. ¹⁴ Make yourself an ark of gopherwood; make rooms in the ark, and cover it inside and outside with pitch."*

Genesis 6:17- 18 (NKJV) – *"¹⁷ And behold, I Myself am bringing floodwaters on the earth, to destroy from under heaven all flesh in which is the breath of life; everything that is on the earth shall die. ¹⁸ But I will establish My covenant with you; and you shall go into the ark—you, your sons, your wife, and your sons' wives with you."*

Genesis 7:5 (NKJV) *"And Noah did all that the Lord commanded him.*

Genesis 7:16 (NKJV) *"So those that entered, male and female of all flesh, went in as God had commanded him; and the LORD shut him in."*

Genesis 8:20 (NKJV) *"Then Noah built an altar to the LORD, and took of every clean animal and of every clean bird, and offered burnt offerings on the altar."*

24. JOSEPH

(The Choice to Rise Above Past Pain and Betrayal and Forgive Those Who Sought to Kill Your Destiny)

Joseph found himself in the place of distress, when his brothers become jealous of him because of the favour he enjoyed from his father, and they conspired to throw him in a pit, then they decided to sell him as a slave. His distress continued while working at Potipher's house when Potipher's wife decided falsely accuse him of immorality and he was thrown in prison.

However, Joseph's decision to remain calm and to trust in God's ability to deliver him and vindicate him, plus his generous use of his gifts to help other distressed people who were in prison with him, is what ushered him and propelled him into a place of destiny as the second in command in Pharaoh's palace. Joseph went on to become the one to salvage his brothers from their place of famine and distress.

Sometimes we may suffer injustices, persecutions and oppression from those who seek to kill our destiny and we may find ourselves in places of distress out of no fault of our own.

Our ability to trust God and wait on him to deliver us from those situations and more so our ability to remain faithfully focused, without murmuring or complaining or backsliding, is what will testify in our favour and move us from distress to destiny.

Joseph's ability to forgive his brothers for having tried to kill him and his destiny is a key lesson in moving from distress to destiny because it is when we have reached our mountain top in terms of success, influential positions, material wealth, ministerial success etc. that we face our greatest tests in terms of how we handle people who might have offended us or hurt us along the way. It is important to note Joseph's reasoning as to what motivated him to forgive his brothers namely, the fact that God had been with him throughout and blessed him and lifted him despite the attempts by his brother to derail him from destiny. This is indeed a mark of maturity that will often move us from distress to destiny.

Genesis 37:23-24 (NKJV) *"So it came to pass, when Joseph had come to his brothers, that they stripped Joseph of his tunic, the tunic of many colors that was on him. Then they took him and cast him into a pit. And the pit was empty; there was no water in it."*

Genesis 37:27-28 (NKJV) *"27 Come and let us sell him to the Ishmaelites, and let not our hand be upon him, for he is our brother and our flesh." And his brothers listened. 28 Then Midianite traders passed by; so the brothers pulled Joseph up and lifted him out of the pit, and sold him to the Ishmaelites for twenty shekels of silver. And they took Joseph to Egypt."*

Genesis 39:6-8 (NKJV) *"6 Thus he left all that he had in Joseph's hand, and he did not know what he had except for the bread which he ate. Now Joseph was handsome in form and appearance. 7 And it came to pass after these things that his master's wife cast longing eyes on Joseph, and she said, "Lie with me." 8 But he refused and said to his master's wife, "Look, my master does not know what is* *with me in the house, and he has committed all that he has to my hand."*

Genesis 39:12-14 (NKJV) *"[12] that she caught him by his garment, saying, "Lie with me." But he left his garment in her hand, and fled and ran outside. [13] And so it was, when she saw that he had left his garment in her hand and fled outside, [14] that she called to the men of her house and spoke to them, saying, "See, he has brought in to us a Hebrew to [a]mock us. He came in to me to lie with me, and I cried out with a loud voice. [15] And it happened, when he heard that I lifted my voice and cried out, that he left his garment with me, and fled and went outside."*

Genesis 50:19-21 (NKJV) *"[19] Joseph said to them, "Do not be afraid, for am I in the place of God? [20] But as for you, you meant evil against me; but God meant it for good, in order to bring it about as it is this day, to save many people alive. [21] Now therefore, do not be afraid; I will provide for you and your little ones." And he comforted them and spoke kindly to them."*

25. JOB

(The Choice to Refuse to Curse God Even When You Feel He Has Forsaken You)

Job is a classic case of one who was faithful and righteous, yet he suffered great distress through his health, loss of his properties, death of his children, but in all that he refused to curse God and he chose to trust God's mercies and God's faithfulness.

God eventually delivered Job from his **distress** and moved him on to his **destiny**, after teaching him some crucial lessons that are so valuable to us today when we go through our *"Job Seasons"*

Our journey to destiny is not a bed of roses and we will suffer, make sacrifices and incur great losses, but it is our ability to remain in

God, that will usher us out of those distresses into our places of destiny, where those sacrifices and losses will be so insignificant in the light of great gain and restoration that awaits us ahead.

Like Job, when Jesus was in great distress in the Garden of Gethsemane, He also refused to blame God, and He chose to endure His distress knowing that ultimately after serving the purposes of God, He would be propelled to fulfil his destiny which was to redeem mankind.

Sometimes our seasons of distress are intended to serve God's plan and our ability to persevere and endure and allow the will of God to prevail over our own will is what will qualify us for destiny.

Job 1:20-21 (NKJV) *"20 Then Job arose, tore his robe, and shaved his head; and he fell to the ground and worshiped. 21 And he said: "Naked I came from my mother's womb, And naked shall I return there. The Lord gave, and the Lord has taken away; Blessed be the name of the Lord."*

Job 2:9-10 (NKJV) *9 Then his wife said to him, "Do you still hold fast to your integrity? Curse God and die!" 10 But he said to her, "You speak as one of the foolish women speaks. Shall we indeed accept good from God, and shall we not accept adversity?" In all this Job did not sin with his lips."*

Job 42:10-11 (NKJV) *"10 And the Lord restored Job's losses when he prayed for his friends. Indeed, the Lord gave Job twice as much as he had before. 11 Then all his brothers, all his sisters, and all those who had been his acquaintances before, came to him and ate food with him in his house; and they consoled him and comforted him for all the adversity that the Lord had brought upon him. Each one gave him a piece of silver and each a ring of gold."*

26. JONAH

(The Choice to Resist or Surrender to the Will of God)

Jonah found himself at a place of distress when he sought to disobey God's instructions and he ended up trying to escape, but when he was thrown overboard, he found himself in even greater distress when he was swallowed by the whale.

Fortunately, the three days that Jonah was in the belly of the whale, he had time to reflect and realised that he could escape from God's Call and when he decided to obey God, God delivered him out of the belly of the whale.

However, Jonah found himself in distress again, when he got angry because God forgave the people, Jonah had been sent to warn of destruction.

When we question God's ways, motives, and intentions or when we murmur as God shows mercy towards others (who we feel are not deserving of his mercies) it means that we have become arrogant, hard hearted and we will remain in a place of distress.

Our duty is to obey God's instructions and leave the outcome to him.

Jonah 1:1-3 (NKJV) *"Now the word of the Lord came to Jonah the son of Amittai, saying, ² "Arise, go to Nineveh, that great city, and cry out against it; for their wickedness has come up before Me." ³ But Jonah arose to flee to Tarshish from the presence of the Lord. He went down to Joppa, and found a ship going to Tarshish; so he paid the fare, and went down into it, to go with them to Tarshish from the presence of the Lord."*

Jonah 2:1-2 (NKJV) *"hen Jonah prayed to the Lord his God from the fish's belly. ² And he said: "I cried out to the Lord because of my affliction, And He answered me. "Out of the belly of Sheol I cried, And You heard my voice."*

Jonah 2:7 (NKJV) *"When my soul fainted within me, I remembered the Lord; And my prayer went up to You, Into Your holy temple."*

Jonah 3:3 (NKJV) *"So Jonah arose and went to Nineveh..."*

Jonah 4:1-2 (NKJV) *"But it displeased Jonah exceedingly, and he became angry. ² So he prayed to the LORD, and said, Ah, LORD, was not this what I said when I was still in my country? Therefore, I fled previously to Tarshish; for I know that You are a gracious and merciful God, slow to anger and abundant in lovingkindness, one who relents from doing harm."*

27. ISAAC

(The Choice To Sow Abundantly In Your Seasons Of Lack)

Isaac was the son of Abraham and he found himself in distress in a foreign land called Gerar during a time of famine.

However, his radical decision to sow abundantly in a time of famine gave him a hundred-fold harvest that moved him from that distress towards his destiny.

Sometimes when we suffer distress in our finances, and we find ourselves in a dry season of lack, either due to business collapse, bankruptcy, wrong investments, etc. we may need to take radical steps by radical faith and release and let go of whatever we may have and sow it during that difficult time in order to provoke a radical harvest. This is why our faithfulness in our giving and offerings is so important especially when we give out of our lack because that kind of giving is deeply sacrificial and it comes out of a place of deep faith in God's faithfulness to provide for us.

Genesis 26:2-3; 6 (NKJV) *"There was a famine in the land, besides the first famine that was in the days of Abraham. And Isaac went to Abimelech king of the Philistines, in Gerar.² Then the Lord appeared to him and said: "Do not go down to Egypt; live in the land of which I shall tell you. ³ Dwell in this land, and I will be with you and bless you; for to you and your descendants I give all these lands, and I will perform the oath which I swore to Abraham your father… ⁶ So Isaac dwelt in Gerar."*

Genesis 26:12 (NKJV) *"Then Isaac sowed in that land, and reaped in the same year a hundredfold; and the LORD blessed him."*

Mark.12:42-44 (NKJV) *"⁴² Then one poor widow came and threw in two mites, which make a quadrans. ⁴³ So He called His disciples to Himself and said to them, "Assuredly, I say to you that this poor widow has put in more than all those who have given to the treasury; ⁴⁴ for they all put in out of their abundance, but she out of her poverty put in all that she had, her whole livelihood."*

28. JOCHEBED

(The Choice to Place the Destiny of Your Child Above Your Own Safety)

Jochebed was Moses' mother who found herself in a place of distress after she bore her baby Moses and Pharaoh was out to kill every Hebrew baby boy. So Jochebed devised a strategy whereby she placed her baby in a basket and put him in a river bank that someone would find him and save his life. Jochebed must have discerned that she had birthed a destiny child that would be used of God greatly. She was a preserver of the move of God, because indeed Moses later manifested into a great move of God who was used to deliver the children of Israel from bondage and slavery in Egypt.

Jochebed's radical decision to save her son's life by willing to risk the possibility of being caught and killed by Pharoah was sacrificial.

Her distress ended when by God's grace her strategy to also become the baby's nurse also paid off when Pharaoh's daughter adopted Moses even though she had to endure the pain of hearing another woman claim ownership of her son.

Sometimes we may need to make very painful choices and decisions whether as parents, business owners, leaders, and servants of God in order to allow God to workout situations in our lives and move us from distress.

It will also require us to operate in divine strategies, and deep godly wisdom to survive the risks involved in those radical choices.

Exodus 13:15-17 (NKJV) *"15 And it came to pass, when Pharaoh was stubborn about letting us go, that the Lord killed all the firstborn in the land of Egypt, both the firstborn of man and the firstborn of beast. Therefore I sacrifice to the Lord all males that open the womb, but all the firstborn of my sons I redeem.' 16 It shall be as a sign on your hand and as frontlets between your eyes, for by strength of hand the Lord brought us out of Egypt." 17 Then it came to pass, when Pharaoh had let the people go, that God did not lead them by way of the land of the Philistines, although that was near; for God said, "Lest perhaps the people change their minds when they see war, and return to Egypt."*

Exodus.2:2-4 (NKJV) *"2 So the woman conceived and bore a son. And when she saw that he was a beautiful child, she hid him three months. 3 But when she could no longer hide him, she took an ark of bulrushes for him, daubed it with asphalt and pitch, put the child in it, and laid it in the reeds by the river's bank. 4 And his sister stood afar off, to know what would be done to him."*

Exodus. 2:7-9 (NKJV) "⁷ Then his sister said to Pharaoh's daughter, "Shall I go and call a nurse for you from the Hebrew women, that she may nurse the child for you?" ⁸ And Pharaoh's daughter said to her, "Go." So, the maiden went and called the child's mother. ⁹ Then Pharaoh's daughter said to her, "Take this child away and nurse him for me, and I will give you your wages." So, the woman took the child and nursed him."

Exodus 3:2-5 (NKJV) "² And the Angel of the Lord appeared to him in a flame of fire from the midst of a bush. So, he looked, and behold, the bush was burning with fire, but the bush was not consumed. ³ Then Moses said, "I will now turn aside and see this great sight, why the bush does not burn." ⁴ So when the Lord saw that he turned aside to look, God called to him from the midst of the bush and said, "Moses, Moses!" And he said, "Here I am." ⁵ Then He said, "Do not draw near this place. Take your sandals off your feet, for the place where you stand is holy ground." ⁶ Moreover He said, "I am the God of your father—the God of Abraham, the God of Isaac, and the God of Jacob." And Moses hid his face, for he was afraid to look upon God."

Exodus 3:9-10 (NKJV) "⁹ Now therefore, behold, the cry of the children of Israel has come to Me, and I have also seen the oppression with which the Egyptians oppress them. ¹⁰ Come now, therefore, and I will send you to Pharaoh that you may bring My people, the children of Israel, out of Egypt."

29. HANNAH

(The Choice to Press and Travail for the Best that God Has for You and to Refuse to Settle for Less)

Hannah was in an extreme place of distress, when she could not bear children and she suffered distress when her husband in his ignorance kept trying to persuade her to be satisfied with him and forget about bearing children.

However deep-down Hannah know that God had created her for more and that she would be a carrier of a destiny child who would become a radical game changer as God used him to bring transformation in the Nation of Israel.

So, Hannah made a radical decision to press in and travail at the place of worship until God broke her barrenness.

Like Hannah, we must refuse to settle for less and press on to lay hold of the best that God has for us.

In addition, Hannah also made a radical vow that touched the heart of God and ushered her from her distress to her destiny.

1st Samuel 1:8 (NKJV) *"Then Elkanah her husband said to her, "Hannah, why do you weep? Why do you not eat? And why is your heart grieved? Am I not better to you than ten sons?"*

1st Samuel 1:6-7 (NKJV) *"⁶ And her rival also provoked her severely, to make her miserable, because the Lord had closed her womb. ⁷ So it was, year by year, when she went up to the house of the Lord, that she provoked her; therefore, she wept and did not eat."*

1st Samuel 1:10-11 (NKJV) *"¹⁰ And she was in bitterness of soul, and prayed to the Lord and [h]wept in anguish. ¹¹ Then she made a vow and said, "O Lord of hosts, if You will indeed look on the affliction of Your maidservant and remember me, and not forget Your maidservant, but will give Your maidservant a male child, then I will give him to the Lord all the days of his life, and no razor shall come upon his head."*

1st Samuel 1:17 (NKJV) *"¹⁷ Then Eli answered and said, "Go in peace, and the God of Israel grant your petition which you have asked of Him."*

30. HEZEKIAH

(The Choice to Reject Death When You Feel that You Have not Quite Fulfilled Your Purpose)

When God told Hezekiah a time had come so put his house in order because he was going to die. He found himself in a place of great distress.

However, Hezekiah made a radical decision to plead bitterly to God to extend his life by reminding God how he walked in truth, how loyal he had been to him, and how he consistently did good in the sight of the Lord. Then God heard his prayer and extended his life for fifteen more years.

Sometimes we may need to negotiate with God when we are faced with life threatening situations such as sickness, life of loved ones.

Sometimes when we know we are about to die, we may have regrets by feeling that we did not accomplish or fulfil fundamental things that we ought to have accomplished and fulfilled especially in terms of our purpose and calling, and we may see the need to negotiate with God and beseech him to preserve us and give us more time in order to fulfil that which we have not fulfilled, but we make this request at our own risk especially where after God has mercy on us and gives us an extended grace period we fail to keep our word and we waste those extended years.

This is what happened to Hezekiah because after he requested and God granted him the extension of 15 years, instead of using that time to do good and fulfil God's plan and agenda, he unfortunately ended up missing it.

One at stake, threat of job loss or property, being mortgaged, when we are falsely accused and may be imprisoned among other challenging circumstances. We end up remind God of our good deeds and our righteous walk and bargain for our own good and seek God's mercies.

2nd Kings.20:1-6 (NKJV) – *"In those days Hezekiah was sick and near death. And Isaiah the prophet, the son of Amoz, went to him and said to him, "Thus says the* LORD: *'Set your house in order, for you shall die, and not live.' ² Then he turned his face toward the wall, and prayed to the* LORD, *saying, ³ "Remember now, O* LORD, *I pray, how I have walked before You in truth and with a loyal heart, and have done what was good in Your sight." And Hezekiah wept bitterly. ⁴ And it happened, before Isaiah had gone out into the middle court, that the word of the* LORD *came to him, saying, ⁵ "Return and tell Hezekiah the leader of My people, 'Thus says the* LORD, *the God of David your father: "I have heard your prayer, I have seen your tears; surely, I will heal you. On the third day you shall go up to the house of the* LORD. *⁶ And I will add to your days fifteen years..."*

2nd King 20:12-19 (NKJV) – *¹² At that time Berodach-Baladan the son of Baladan, king of Babylon, sent letters and a present to Hezekiah, for he heard that Hezekiah had been sick. ¹³ And Hezekiah was attentive to them, and showed them all the house of his treasures— the silver and gold, the spices and precious ointment, and [d]all [e] his armoury—all that was found among his treasures. There was nothing in his house or in all his dominion that Hezekiah did not show them. ¹⁴ Then Isaiah the prophet went to King Hezekiah, and said to him, "What did these men say, and from where did they come to you?" So, Hezekiah said, "They came from a far country, from Babylon." ¹⁵ And he said, "What have they seen in your house?" So, Hezekiah answered, "They have seen all that is in my house; there is nothing among my treasures that I have not shown them." ¹⁶ Then Isaiah said to Hezekiah, "Hear the word of the Lord: ¹⁷ 'Behold, the days are coming when all that is in your house, and what your fathers have accumulated until this day, shall be carried to Babylon;*

nothing shall be left,' says the Lord. [18] *'And they shall take away some of your sons who will descend from you, whom you will beget; and they shall be eunuchs in the palace of the king of Babylon.' "* [19] *So Hezekiah said to Isaiah, "The word of the Lord which you have spoken is good!" For he said, "Will there not be peace and truth at least in my days?"*

2nd Kings 20:20-21 (NKJV) *"* [20] *Now the rest of the acts of Hezekiah—all his might, and how he made a pool and a tunnel and brought water into the city—are they not written in the book of the chronicles of the kings of Judah?* [21] *So Hezekiah rested with his fathers. Then Manasseh his son reigned in his place."*

Bibliography

The Bible

Rao, Hari.2015. *6 Signs You are a True Spiritual.* On accessed on 5th Nov 2020 https://www.getreadyministry.com/6-signs-you-are-a-true-spiritual-son/

Onoriobe, Israel. 2019. *Characteristics & Benefits of the Father Son Relationship,* accessed on 5th Nov 2020 https://www.wvcom-international.org/characteristics-benefits-of-the-father-son-relationship/

Kail, Jake. 2015. *Characteristics of Spiritual Father* accessed on 5th Nov 2020https://jakekail.com/4-characteristics-spiritual-fathers/

Farley, William. 2020. *How to Be a Spiritual Father* accessed on 5th Nov 2020https://www.desiringgod.org/articles/how-to-be a-spiritual-father

Cooke, Tony. 2019. *Ten Traits of Spiritual Fathers* (According to Paul) accessed on https://www.tonycooke.org/articles-by-tony cooke/ten-traits-sspiritual-fathers/

Jakes, T.D. 2007. *Reposition Yourself Reflections: Living Life Without Limits.* Atria Books.

Wairimu, Teresa. 2011. *A Cactus in the Desert.* Rev Teresia Wairimu Kinyanjui.

Mbugua, Judy. 2002. *A Second Chance. Authentic Lifestyle*

Wilkinson, Bruce. 2000. *The Prayer Of Jabez: Breaking through to the Blessed Life.* Multnomah Publishers

Munroe, Myles. 2008. *Becoming A Leader Workbook.* Whitaker House

White, Jerry. 1996. *The Power of Commitment: How Ordinary People Can Make an Extraordinary Impact on the World* (Life and Ministry of Jesus Christ). NavPress

Yancey, Philip. 2010. *Where Is God When It Hurts?* Zondervan; Anniversary edition

Wiersbe, Warren. 2006. *The Bumps Are What You Climb On*: Encouragement for Difficult Days. Revell

Tenney, Tommy. 1998. *The God Chasers: My Soul Follows Hard After Thee.* Destiny Image Publishers

Joyner, Rick. 2007. *The Harvest.* Morningstar Publications (NC)